2025

Awakening Intelligence

A Journey into the World of AI

Mohamed Fawzi Elgendi

www.fawzooz.ai

Book Title: Awakening Intelligence

Author's Name: Mohammed Fawzi Elgendi

Publisher: Self-published (fawzooz.ai)

Address: Al Qouz Creative Zone, Dubai, United Arab Emirates

Book Language: English

Category: Applied Sciences (Technology)

Publishing Printing & Text Permit: MC-01-01-7474350

ISBN: 9789948707479

Age Classification : E

"The age group suitable for the book's content has been classified and determined according to the age classification system issued by the UAE Media Council"

Printed by: Ingram content group

Lightning Source FZC LLC, Sharjah Publishing City

United Arab Emirates

COPYRIGHT

To the awakening intelligence,

both within machines and within ourselves.

TABLE OF CONTENT

INTRODUCTION

Towards a better world

My journey into the world of Artificial Intelligence began with skepticism. Like many, I saw AI as a distant, futuristic concept – all hype and no practical application. But as I delved deeper, I discovered something remarkable: AI isn't just about building intelligent machines, it's about enhancing our own intelligence and reshaping the world around us.

We stand at the cusp of an AI revolution, a moment where the science of intelligent machines intersects with the very essence of human experience. But what kind of intelligence are we building? How can we ensure that AI serves humanity, enhances our capabilities, and upholds our values? This book explores these critical questions, reminding us that the true power of AI lies not just in its algorithms, but in its ability to amplify human potential.

Imagine a world where machines not only think, but also understand, collaborate, and create alongside humans. This isn't science fiction – it's the promise of Artificial Intelligence. But how do we awaken this intelligence responsibly? How do we ensure that AI becomes a force for good, a partner in our progress? This book is a guide to navigating this uncharted territory, to understanding the science behind AI and the ethical considerations that must guide its development.

This book is an invitation to join me on that journey, to move beyond the hype and discover the true potential of AI.

CHAPTER 1

From Skeptic to Advocate

"AI is just hype, until it changes everything you do."

For many of us, the journey into Artificial Intelligence (AI) begins with a healthy dose of skepticism. After all, it's easy to doubt sweeping claims about machines "outsmarting" humans or revolutionizing entire industries overnight. Yet, as you peel back the layers of AI, you discover that it's not about replacing people, it's about enhancing our capabilities and reshaping how we live and work. This is the story of how I went from doubting AI's utility to becoming one of its most passionate advocates.

1.1 The Early Doubts

When I first heard about AI, my mind jumped to Hollywood portrayals: robot overlords, sentient machines, and other futuristic fantasies. Meanwhile, in reality, many AI applications were mundane like spam filters, basic recommendation engines, or simple chatbots. I questioned whether AI was really the next big thing or just another passing trend.

1.2 Three Statements to Reflect On

During the early phase of my learning, three statements stood out:

- "AI is just hype, until it changes everything you do."
- "Every business decision can be enhanced by better data and better predictions."
- "Humans must remain at the heart of AI to ensure it serves us ethically and productively."

I came across these ideas in my very first AI-focused sessions, and they served as constant reminders that skepticism could evolve into genuine curiosity and appreciationprovided I kept an open mind.

1.3 Embracing the Need for Change

As industries continued to automate routine tasks, it became clear that AI and Machine Learning (ML) were driving these changes. I realized there was a gap in my own skill set: I knew how to interpret data at a surface level but lacked the deeper understanding of algorithms or how to embed AI into business strategies.

- **Self-Education**: I began taking courses and attending workshops to grasp the fundamentals of AI, ML, and data science.
- **Hands-On Practice**: Implementing small projects like (building a basic sentiment-analysis tool) helped me see AI as approachable and deeply impactful.
- **Collaborative Learning**: Engaging with a community of fellow learners and AI professionals accelerated my transition from "skeptic" to "enthusiast."

1.4 The Transformation Moment

The real turning point was when I participated in a project that aimed to predict pneumonia using X-ray images. By analyzing medical image data - such as tissue patterns and density level - I developed a predictive model powered by artificial intelligence that accurately identified potential cases of pneumonia.

Using AI-driven insights, the system enabled doctors to diagnose cases more quickly and efficiently, leading to faster treatment and reducing the risk of disease progression. Watching these predictions translate into real-world impact was eye-opening. It wasn't just about exploring AI's novelty; it was about solving meaningful problems. This success story captured everything that had once been a theoretical promise of "AI potential" and turned it into a practical, life-saving application.

1.5 Why AI Advocacy Matters

After witnessing what AI could do, I became more vocal about its benefits. Here's why advocacy is so critical:

- **Closing the Knowledge Gap**: Misconceptions and fear often hinder AI adoption. Advocates can demystify AI, showing it as a tool to augment - not replace - human intelligence.
- **Driving Ethical Practices**: When more people understand how AI works, there's greater accountability. Questions around bias, privacy, and transparency come to the forefront, ensuring AI evolves responsibly.
- **Fostering Innovation**: An organization that embraces AI can dramatically speed up its innovation cycle. Advocates help steer conversations around priorities, ensuring technology adoption aligns with business goals.

1.6 Bridging Skepticism and Pragmatism

Being a skeptic initially served as an advantage. It forced me to question real-world applicability and demand tangible evidence of AI's worth. Once I saw that proof - like predicting customer churn, optimizing inventory, and improving user experiences - my perspective shifted.

- **Healthy Doubt → Constructive Critique**: Skeptics can play a vital role in refining AI solutions by challenging assumptions.
- **Pragmatic Acceptance**: Realizing AI's constraints is as important as championing its possibilities. Not every problem requires a complex deep learning model; sometimes a simpler approach suffices.

1.7 Looking Ahead

This book begins with a personal story of skepticism turning into belief. As we delve deeper, you'll see that AI is more than just lines of code or theoretical models, it's a new lens through which we can tackle age-old problems. From enhancing product recommendations and automating tedious tasks, to discovering life-saving medical insights, AI's potential is limited only by our willingness to engage, learn, and collaborate.

In the next chapters, we'll explore the nuances of AI from human intelligence and emotional factors to the broader wonders of AI perception, inference, decision-making, and creativity. We'll also address practical aspects like data readiness, organizational strategy, and the ethical considerations that ensure AI remains a force for positive transformation.

Consider this chapter your invitation to journey from skeptic to advocate and beyond.

Key Takeaways

- **AI Skepticism Is Normal**: Doubt often signals a need for deeper exploration.
- **Real Use Cases Change Minds**: Practical applications and measurable outcomes have the power to shift perspectives dramatically.
- **Ethics and Humans at the Center**: AI should serve to enhance human work and well-being, not undermine it.
- **Evolving Mindset**: The transition from skeptic to advocate is an ongoing process of learning, testing, and real-world validation.

Your own transformation journey might look different, but the underlying principle remains: once you see AI's tangible impact, it's hard to remain a skeptic. The world of AI is vast, and understanding its foundational principles will prepare you to harness its power responsibly and effectively.

CHAPTER 2

Human Intelligence and Why AI Matters

"AI intelligence, when guided by human emotional insight, becomes a powerful tool to understand, connect, and enhance human potential."

AI stands for "Artificial Intelligence," but the term alone can overshadow an important truth: *not all intelligence is artificial, nor should it be.* Before diving into the core mechanics of AI (its algorithms, data requirements, and applications) it's crucial to recognize the value of human intelligence and why AI amplifies, rather than replaces, our innate abilities.

In this chapter, we'll explore the various forms of human intelligence, the role of emotional intelligence (EQ) in an AI-driven world, and how humans and AI can complement one another. By understanding these dynamics, you'll see why AI matters and how it can serve as a powerful ally in both personal and professional spheres.

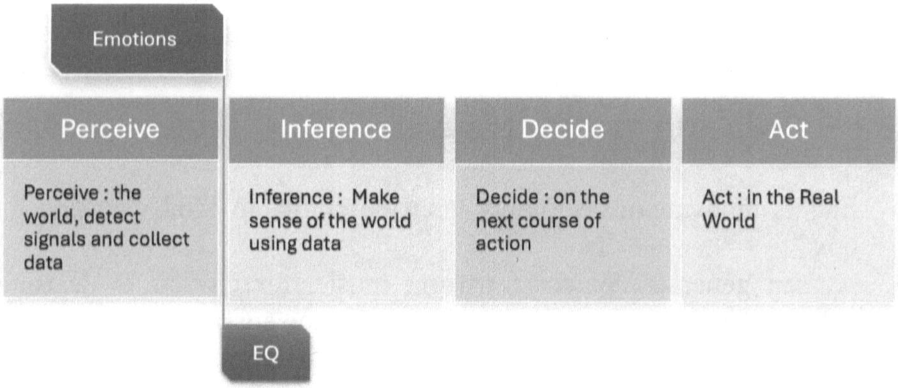

*Figure 1: Categories of Human Intelligence**

**"This structure/shape was developed based on concepts/ideas that were reviewed during an Industry session in the post graduate program in AI for Leaders (UT Austin McCombs / Great Learning)."*

2.1 The Many Faces of Human Intelligence

Human intelligence is multifaceted, ranging from the analytical to the emotional, from the creative to the social. Recognizing this breadth is the first step to understanding what AI can and cannot replicate (at least for now).

2.1.1 Analytical Intelligence (IQ)

- Focuses on logic, reasoning, and problem-solving skills.
- Often measured by standardized tests and is closely linked to academic performance.
- AI can emulate certain aspects (like pattern recognition and data-driven solutions) but struggles with context that involves social or emotional nuance.

2.1.2 Emotional Intelligence (EQ)

- Involves self-awareness, empathy, motivation, and managing interpersonal relationships.
- Vital in leadership, teamwork, and customer-facing roles.
- While AI can analyze emotional sentiment in text or speech, it does not experience emotions in the human sense. Empathy and genuine connection remain uniquely human.

2.1.3 Creative Intelligence

- Entails innovation, originality, and the ability to think "outside the box."
- AI can generate content (artwork, music, text) often by learning patterns from massive datasets. However, the spark of creativity that aligns with human culture and emotional resonance still largely depends on human input and curation.

2.1.4 Practical Intelligence

- Deals with real-world problem-solving skills and adaptability.

- People develop it through experience, social interactions, and hands-on learning.
- AI can assist by providing data-driven insights, but the intuition to decide how to apply these insights effectively often rests with humans.

By understanding these forms of intelligence, we begin to see the synergy that arises when humans and AI work together: AI handles repetitive or data-heavy tasks, freeing humans to focus on creativity, empathy, leadership, and nuanced decision-making.

2.2 The Intersection of Human and Machine Intelligence

2.2.1 Beyond Automation

A common misconception is that AI's primary purpose is to automate jobs and replace workers. In reality, many successful AI implementations focus on *augmentation*: using AI to assist professionals with tasks that can be tedious or error-prone for humans. For example:

- **Healthcare**: AI-powered diagnostic tools can analyze medical images with high precision, but medical professionals still make final judgments and provide empathetic patient care.
- **Customer Service**: Chatbots handle FAQs and repetitive queries, while human agents step in for complex, emotionally charged interactions.

2.2.2 The Role of Data

AI thrives on data. Large, quality datasets feed algorithms, enabling them to learn, adapt, and predict. Meanwhile, humans excel at interpreting results and asking the "why" behind the data. A machine might predict a stock price drop based on patterns, but it's often a human who spots an anomaly (e.g., a sudden geopolitical shift) that the model never learned to account for.

2.2.3 Emotions as a Human Differentiator

Emotions guide our decisions in ways that data points alone cannot capture. While AI can detect sentiment in text or voice, the genuine emotional connection - the ability to console, encourage, or inspire - remains largely the domain of humans. In business contexts, empathy can build trust with customers or team members, leading to better relationships and outcomes.

2.3 Why AI Matters in the Modern World

So, if human intelligence is so valuable, why does AI matter? The short answer: *Scale, speed, and efficiency.* Here are a few reasons AI has become a driving force in modern enterprises:

- **Complexity Management:** Today's business problems often involve hundreds of variables and massive data sets. AI algorithms can process these at speeds impossible for humans, unearthing insights that might otherwise remain hidden.
- **Precision and Consistency:** Humans get tired, distracted, or biased. AI models, once trained correctly, can maintain a consistent level of performance without fatigue, offering reliable support for tasks like quality control in manufacturing or anomaly detection in cybersecurity.
- **Accelerated Innovation:** Access to real-time insights enables faster and more informed decision-making. Whether launching new products or optimizing supply chains, AI shortens the feedback loop between experimentation and results.
- **Enhancement of Human Roles:** By handling repetitive tasks, AI allows people to focus on jobs that require critical thinking, empathy, and creative problem-solving - areas where humans hold a distinct advantage.

2.4 The Evolving Landscape: AI Meets EQ

2.4.1 Future-Proofing Your Skill Set

As AI becomes more capable in tasks that once required analytical skills, the ability to understand and manage human emotions is increasingly valuable. Strengthening emotional intelligence (EQ) and interpersonal skills is a way to *future-proof* yourself or your organization.

- **Leadership**: Inspiring and guiding teams through change.
- **Communication**: Explaining complex decisions to stakeholders in a relatable manner.
- **Empathy**: Building products, services, and solutions that resonate with people's needs.

2.4.2 AI-Assisted Coaching and Self-Improvement

Interestingly, AI can support the development of emotional intelligence. For example, AI-driven coaching platforms can analyze your communication style (spoken or written) and provide insights into your tone, word choice, and how others might perceive them. The combination of *human reflection* on AI-driven feedback can spur personal and professional growth.

2.5 AI and Humanity: A Symbiotic Relationship

Rather than viewing AI as an adversary, it's more accurate to see it as an *ally* that can help us unlock new levels of productivity and creativity. Here's how:

- **Collaborative Decision-Making:** AI offers recommendations based on massive data sets. Human experts then apply domain knowledge and emotional intelligence to refine and finalize decisions.
  Example: In financial services, AI might flag potential investment strategies, but humans weigh client goals, risk tolerance, and market sentiment to pick the best course.
- **Continuous Learning:** AI systems learn over time from new data, while humans learn from direct experiences and social interactions. Combining these learning modes can drive innovations across industries, from manufacturing to healthcare and beyond.
- **Elevated Customer Experiences:** Chatbots and virtual assistants handle routine tasks, but humans can step in for personalized interactions that require empathy. Together, they form a robust support system that balances efficiency with genuine connection.

2.6 Looking Ahead to the Next Chapters

Understanding human intelligence sets the stage for everything that follows in this book. It clarifies the distinct strengths that humans bring to the table - empathy, judgment, creativity - while highlighting the areas where AI can excel - large-scale data analysis, pattern recognition, and consistent execution.

In the next chapters, we'll explore how AI processes information (like perceiving images, text, and speech), how it infers patterns, and how it can even participate in creative tasks. We'll also examine the different types of AI (from simple optimization to more sophisticated decision-making) and dive into the concept of AI maturity - a roadmap for businesses transitioning from novice to advanced AI practitioners.

This foundation in human intelligence underscores a central theme you'll revisit again and again: AI is not a substitute for human genius, but a catalyst that, when harnessed responsibly, can elevate human potential.

Key Takeaways

- **Human Intelligence Is Multifaceted**: Analytical IQ, emotional EQ, creativity, and practical problem-solving are all crucial forms of intelligence. AI mimics some aspects but not the totality of human cognition.
- **AI Augments, Not Replaces**: The best AI applications enhance human capabilities - managing complex data tasks so humans can focus on empathy, creativity, and strategic thinking.
- **EQ in an AI World**: Emotional intelligence becomes more valuable as AI grows more adept at analytical tasks, underscoring the importance of skills like empathy and communication.
- **Why AI Matters**: AI delivers speed, scalability, and consistency, helping manage ever-expanding data and complexity in modern business environments.
- **Symbiosis Over Competition**: Humans and AI work best in tandem, where each complements the other's strengths and mitigates the other's weaknesses.

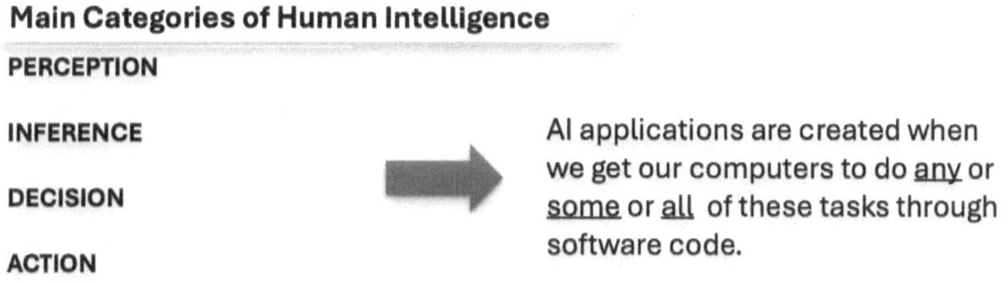

*Figure 2: AI applications types**

Human intelligence lies at the heart of AI's purpose. By appreciating the diverse strengths humans bring to any challenge, we set the stage for AI to fulfill its role as a powerful, transformative tool - one that can multiply, not replace, the creativity and compassion only we possess.

"This structure/shape was developed based on concepts/ideas that were reviewed during an Industry session in the post graduate program in AI for Leaders (UT Austin McCombs / Great Learning)."

CHAPTER 3

From Basic Definitions to Core Components

"Artificial Intelligence begins as the science of intelligent machines, but it transforms into a powerful force that reshapes our world, awakening us to new possibilities."

By now, you have a sense of how human intelligence and emotional capacity continue to be vital in an AI-driven world. But what exactly is AI, and how do Machine Learning (ML) and Deep Learning (DL) fit into the picture? This chapter aims to clarify key terms, define foundational concepts, and explore how these elements come together to power modern AI systems.

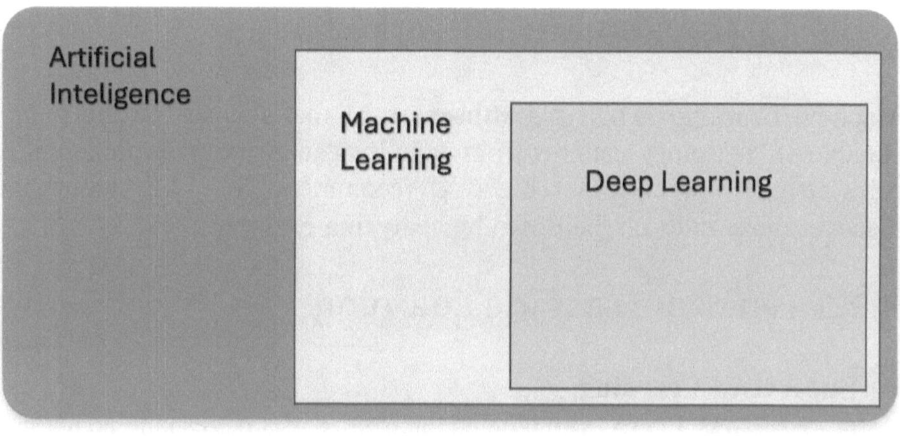

Figure 3: AI & ML

3.1 Defining Artificial Intelligence

Artificial Intelligence refers to computer systems or algorithms that mimic - or exceed - human cognitive tasks such as problem-solving, perception, language understanding, and decision-making. Think of it as a broad umbrella term. Specific AI methods range from simple if-then logic to complex neural networks capable of autonomous learning.

- **Core Objective**: **Automation** of tasks that require some level of intelligence, from filtering spam emails to driving autonomous vehicles.
- **Primary Benefit**: Handling massive volumes of data quickly and consistently, often outperforming humans in speed and accuracy under certain conditions.

3.1.1 Early Milestones in AI

- **Dartmouth Workshop (1956)**: Often cited as the birth of AI as a field, led by John McCarthy, Marvin Minsky, and others.
- **Expert Systems (1980s)**: Symbolic AI systems that captured human expertise in rule-based programs.
- **Neural Networks Revival (1990s–2000s)**: Improved computing power rekindled interest in multi-layer neural networks.

3.2 Understanding Machine Learning

Machine Learning (ML) is a **subset** of AI that focuses on algorithms capable of "learning" patterns from data. Instead of programming explicit rules (e.g., "If a customer buys X, recommend Y"), ML algorithms discover those rules on their own by analyzing examples.

3.2.1 Types of Machine Learning

- **Supervised Learning**
  - **Goal**: Learn from labeled datasets (e.g., images labeled as "cat" or "dog").
  - **Examples**: Email spam detection, credit card fraud detection, image classification.
  - **Common Algorithms**: Linear Regression, Logistic Regression, Decision Trees, Random Forests.
- **Unsupervised Learning**
  - **Goal**: Find structure in unlabeled data (no predefined categories).

    - **Examples**: Customer segmentation, anomaly detection, recommendation clustering.
    - **Common Algorithms**: K-Means Clustering, Principal Component Analysis (PCA), Autoencoders.
- **Semi-Supervised Learning**
    - **Goal**: Leverage a small amount of labeled data plus a larger pool of unlabeled data.
    - **Examples**: Speech recognition with limited transcribed audio, text classification.
    - **Approach**: Uses unsupervised methods to learn data structure, then applies supervised methods on the smaller labeled set.
- **Reinforcement Learning (RL)**
    - **Goal**: Train an agent to make optimal decisions through rewards and penalties.
    - **Examples**: Game-playing AI (chess, Go), robotics navigation.
    - **Approach**: Trial-and-error learning, where the agent explores an environment and is rewarded for beneficial actions.

3.3 Deep Learning: The Powerhouse of Modern AI

Deep Learning (DL) is a **subset** of Machine Learning that uses artificial neural networks with multiple layers - or "deep" architectures - to automatically learn features and patterns from data. While traditional ML often relies on manual feature engineering, DL is designed to learn these features end-to-end.

3.3.1 Key Components of Neural Networks

- **Neurons**: Modeled loosely after biological neurons. Each neuron applies a weight to input data, sums the result, and applies an activation function (like ReLU or sigmoid).
- **Layers**: The network consists of an input layer, multiple hidden layers, and an output layer. Adding more layers often allows the network to capture more complex patterns.
- **Training**: Uses backpropagation, where the network's predictions are compared to the actual labels, and weights are adjusted to minimize error.

3.3.2 Why Deep Learning Is So Effective

- **Automated Feature Extraction**: Instead of manual feature engineering, deep networks learn relevant features from raw data (e.g., pixels, audio waves).
- **Scalability**: With sufficient data and computational power (like GPUs), deep networks can tackle highly complex tasks - e.g., speech recognition, image segmentation, natural language understanding.
- **Transfer Learning**: Pretrained models can transfer their "knowledge" to new tasks, greatly reducing the data needed for training.

3.4 ML vs. DL: When to Use Each

3.4.1 Traditional ML (Shallow Models)

- **Pros**:
    - Works well with limited data.
    - Easier to interpret, especially linear models or small decision trees.
    - Faster to train on standard hardware.
- **Cons**:
    - Requires extensive feature engineering.
    - May not scale effectively with huge datasets.

3.4.2 Deep Learning

- **Pros**:
    - Excellent performance on large, unstructured datasets (images, text, audio).
    - Automated feature learning.
    - State-of-the-art results in many fields (computer vision, natural language processing, etc.).
- **Cons**:
    - Often requires vast amounts of data and computational resources.
    - Harder to interpret ("black box" problem).
    - Prone to overfitting if not managed carefully.

Rule of Thumb: Start with simpler models and progress to deep learning if you have enough data, computational resources, and a complex problem (like image classification or language modeling).

Factor	Machine Learning (ML)	Deep Learning (DL)
Scope	Broad category within AI	Subset of ML
Complexity	Simple models, requires feature extraction	Complex, multi-layered neural networks
Data Dependency	Works well with small to medium datasets	Requires large datasets
Computation	Can run on standard CPUs, less resource-heavy	Requires powerful GPUs, high computational power
Feature Engineering	Manual feature selection	Automatic feature extraction
Examples	Fraud detection, recommendation systems	Image recognition, natural language processing

Figure 4: ML vs dl

3.5 Additional AI Paradigms

While ML and DL dominate much of today's AI discourse, there are additional methods and paradigms:

- **Symbolic AI**
    - Rule-based systems that encode expert knowledge explicitly.
    - Useful for knowledge representation and logic-based reasoning in well-defined domains.
- **Genetic Algorithms (GAs)**
    - Evolutionary approach to optimization, inspired by natural selection.
    - Can be used in design, scheduling, or any problem where we can define a fitness function.
    - **Neuro-Symbolic AI**

- Combines the strengths of symbolic reasoning (explainability, logical structure) with neural networks (pattern recognition, scalability).
- Aim is to get the "best of both worlds": robust reasoning and powerful learning.

3.6 Common Misconceptions About AI

3.6.1 AI Is Just Robots

Robots are one *application* of AI, but AI systems can exist purely in software - e.g., recommendation engines, fraud detection algorithms, and virtual assistants. Physical robotics can use AI to navigate and interact with the environment, but not all AI is tied to robots.

3.6.2 AI Guarantees Intelligent Behavior

AI can appear remarkably intelligent within a narrow domain but be completely inept at tasks outside that domain (this is called "narrow AI"). General Intelligence - akin to human-level adaptability - remains a future challenge (if it's achievable at all, or how soon).

3.6.3 More Data Always Means Better AI

Large datasets are generally beneficial, but data quality matters. If the data is biased, noisy, or irrelevant, more of it won't help. Moreover, the choice of model architecture, hyperparameters, and training approach all significantly influence performance.

3.7 How AI Fits Into the Bigger Picture

AI isn't standalone; it integrates with other technologies and domains to create impactful solutions:

- **Big Data**: Massive datasets stored in distributed systems (like Hadoop, Spark) feed AI algorithms.
- **Cloud Computing**: Flexible, on-demand computational resources for training and deploying AI models.

- **Edge Computing**: AI running on devices with limited resources - like smartphones or IoT sensors - enabling real-time processing.
- **APIs & Services**: Many cloud providers offer AI APIs for tasks like speech-to-text, vision analysis, and language translation, lowering the barrier to entry.

Knowing how these components interact will help you see AI as part of a broader ecosystem, not just a standalone technology.

3.8 Types of Artificial Intelligence

The field of Artificial Intelligence (AI) is evolving at a rapid pace, and with its advancement, different types are being classified based on their capabilities. AI can be broadly divided into three main types:

- **Narrow AI (Weak AI):** This type focuses on performing specific tasks precisely, such as image recognition or language translation. It is the most common type currently and excels in its defined areas, but lacks the ability to generalize beyond them.
- **General AI (Strong AI):** This type aims to create intelligent systems with cognitive abilities similar to humans, capable of understanding and learning any intellectual task that a human can perform. This type is still in its theoretical stages but represents an ambitious goal for researchers.
- **Superintelligent AI:** This type surpasses human intelligence in all aspects, whether creative, scientific, or general. It is a hypothetical concept that raises questions about the future of humanity and its relationship with technology.

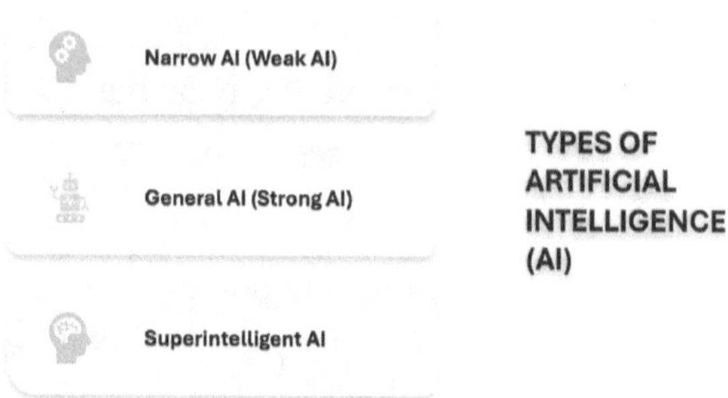

Figure 5: AI types

This classification shows the gradual development of artificial intelligence, from specialized systems to systems that surpass human capabilities. As we advance in this field, it becomes necessary to understand these different types and their potential impacts on our lives and future.

3.9 Preparing for Deeper AI Explorations

In the coming chapters, we'll dive into AI's real-world applications - examining how AI perceives images, text, and speech, performs inference for business decisions, takes action in self-driving vehicles or automated trading, and even engages in creative pursuits like animation or content generation. By solidifying the definitions and frameworks in this chapter, you'll be better equipped to appreciate AI's vast potential and its limitations.

Key Takeaways

- **AI Is Broad**: It encompasses numerous methods - Machine Learning, Deep Learning, symbolic AI, and more - aimed at replicating or surpassing aspects of human cognition.
- **Machine Learning Powers Most Current AI**: ML is about learning from data rather than following strictly hard-coded rules, with DL representing a powerful subfield.
- **Deep Learning Shines with Large, Complex Data**: It can unlock new frontiers in image recognition, speech processing, and NLP, but requires significant resources and faces interpretability challenges.
- **AI Myths Abound**: Recognize that AI isn't always about robots, more data doesn't always mean better performance, and AI excels best in narrowly defined tasks.
- **Integration Is Key**: AI solutions often rely on big data infrastructures, cloud or edge computing, and specialized hardware to deliver real value.

Armed with these insights, you're ready to delve into *how* AI makes sense of the world - perceiving images, text, speech - and making decisions that can transform businesses and industries.

CHAPTER 4

The Wonders of AI

"We're not just building better machines - we're amplifying human potential."

AI's true marvel emerges when we see it in action - spotting anomalies in x-ray scans, predicting consumer behavior, orchestrating self-driving vehicles, or even generating animations that once required painstaking manual labor. These tasks can be loosely grouped into four categories: **perception**, **inference**, **decision-making**, and **creative output**. Each domain highlights how AI has transcended traditional software constraints, enabling transformative solutions across industries.

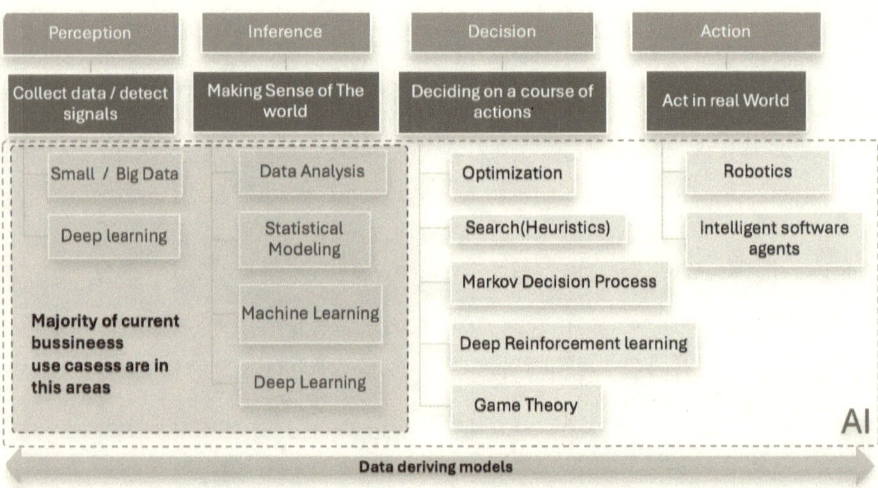

*Figure 6: AI for business enterprise**

**"This structure/shape was developed based on concepts/ideas that were reviewed during an Industry session in the post graduate program in AI for Leaders (UT Austin McCombs / Great Learning)."*

4.1 Perception: How AI Sees, Reads, and Hears

Perception is about interpreting the world through sensory data - images, text, audio. Think of it as giving machines "eyes," "ears," and an ability to "read."

4.1.1 Vision

- **Medical Imaging**: AI-enhanced systems can detect tumors or other anomalies from X-rays, MRIs, or CT scans, often matching or surpassing human radiologists in accuracy.
- **3D Computer Vision**: Used in drones and autonomous vehicles to interpret spatial data for navigation.
- **Edge Computing for Real-Time Processing**: Instead of sending raw footage to the cloud, smart cameras process data locally - critical for scenarios like factory floor monitoring, where low latency is essential.

Why It Matters: Vision AI democratizes expert-level analysis; healthcare professionals can spot issues earlier, and manufacturers can automate defect detection, reducing human error and saving costs.

4.1.2 Text (LLMs - Large Language Models)

- **Document Analysis**: Tools like GPT-based models can summarize legal documents, spot critical clauses, or even generate first drafts of contracts.
- **Sentiment Analysis**: By "reading" social media posts and product reviews, AI gauges public opinion in real time, guiding marketing strategies.
- **Text Summarization**: Large texts - think 100-page reports - can be condensed into executive summaries, enabling faster, more informed decision-making.

Why It Matters: Text-based AI relieves the burden of sifting through endless documents and notes, freeing time for strategic and creative tasks where humans excel.

4.1.3 Speech

- **Speech Recognition**: Systems like Alexa or Google Assistant convert voice commands into actionable requests, bridging humans and machines through natural language.
- **Real-Time Transcription**: Live transcription for meetings, lectures, or interviews enables inclusive communication, especially for individuals who are deaf or hard of hearing.
- **Simultaneous Translation**: AI-driven translation tools break language barriers, facilitating global collaboration.

Why It Matters: As speech interfaces improve, humans spend less time learning "machine languages" and more time interacting with devices as naturally as they would with each other.

4.2 Inference: Extracting Insights from Data

Inference revolves around predicting or classifying based on known data. By analyzing patterns, AI can forecast market trends, anticipate equipment failures, or identify fraudulent transactions.

4.2.1 Banking and Finance

- **Customer Churn Prediction**: AI flags customers likely to close accounts or switch services, allowing for proactive retention strategies.
- **Fraud Detection**: Algorithms spot suspicious transaction patterns, blocking fraudulent activity in near real-time.
- **Risk Assessment**: Lenders and insurers leverage AI to evaluate creditworthiness or claim validity with greater speed and consistency.

4.2.2 Retail and E-Commerce

- **Demand Forecasting**: Historical sales, seasonal data, and social media trends feed models that help retailers optimize inventory, preventing both stockouts and overstock.

- **Personalized Recommendations**: By analyzing browsing and purchasing histories, AI tailors product suggestions, boosting customer satisfaction and revenue.

4.2.3 Industrial and Manufacturing

- **Predictive Maintenance**: Machine sensors generate continuous data on performance, temperature, vibration, etc. AI detects when a part is nearing failure, minimizing costly downtime.
- **Quality Control**: Automated inspections flag defects - like microscopic scratches on semiconductor wafers - faster and more reliably than humans.

Why It Matters: Effective inference reduces guesswork. Organizations can make data-backed decisions, anticipating needs and risks before they become critical, thus improving efficiency and cutting costs.

4.3 Decision & Action: From Autonomous Vehicles to Automated Trading

AI doesn't stop at making predictions; it can also **act** on those predictions. This capability is reshaping industries - logistics, financial markets, and beyond.

4.3.1 Self-Driving Vehicles

- **Logistics**: Companies like Kodiak Robotics develop AI-driven trucks for long-haul routes, enhancing efficiency and safety in the supply chain.
- **Mining and Agriculture**: Autonomous vehicles navigate challenging terrains, reducing risks for human operators and lowering operational costs.

4.3.2 Automated Stock Trading

- **High-Frequency Trading**: Deep reinforcement learning agents buy and sell assets in microseconds, capitalizing on market micro-fluctuations.
- **Portfolio Management**: Algorithms balance risk and reward based on large-scale market analysis and real-time data, providing more precise allocations.

4.3.3 Robotics in Diverse Domains

- **Humanoid Robots**: Machines like Kengoro can perform tasks resembling human labor, from simple assembly work to complex interactions in service industries.
- **Drone Swarms**: Coordinated fleets handle tasks from disaster relief to agricultural monitoring, making split-second decisions based on sensor inputs.

Why It Matters: When AI moves beyond passive recommendation, it can autonomously act on insights - opening doors to efficiency, safety, and performance gains that are simply unattainable through manual processes.

4.4 Creative Tasks: AI as a Muse, Not Just a Tool

Perhaps the most surprising leap is AI's role in creative tasks once thought to be exclusively human domains.

4.4.1 Animation

- **Automating Routine Work**: Tools like DeepMotion and Spline reduce the need for frame-by-frame animation, allowing artists to focus on style and storytelling.
- **3D Character Rigging**: AI can map real-life motion-capture data onto digital characters, speeding up the production pipeline.

4.4.2 Content Writing

- **Blogging and Articles**: AI writers, like ChatGPT or Jasper, help draft pieces, brainstorm headlines, or refine outlines.

- **Copywriting**: Marketers use AI to generate variations of ad copy, rapidly A/B testing to find the most effective messaging.

4.4.3 Graphic Design

- **Layout and Color Matching**: Adobe Sensei and similar AI services suggest design elements or color palettes based on the existing artwork.
- **Quick Mockups**: AI can produce concept sketches, giving designers a starting point to iterate upon.

Why It Matters: AI-driven creativity isn't about replacing human originality; it's a *jumping-off point* - providing templates, ideas, and even entire prototypes. Humans maintain the emotional core and final aesthetic judgment, while AI automates repetitive tasks and sparks new possibilities.

4.5 Making Sense of AI's Breadth

The "wonders of AI" may seem boundless, but they share a common thread: **AI thrives when ample, well-structured data meets powerful algorithms**. Whether it's a camera feed, transactional data, or text documents, AI's ability to observe, learn, and act is only as strong as its data foundation and the context provided by human expertise.

- **Data Quality is Paramount**: Poor data leads to poor results - garbage in, garbage out.
- **Interdisciplinary Collaboration**: Effective AI solutions often require cross-functional teams - from data scientists and domain experts to software engineers and business strategists.

4.6 Looking Ahead

The next question is: *How do we choose the right type of AI system for the task at hand?* That's where we'll move next. Chapter 5 explores **types of AI and the question of "human compassion,"** examining tasks that call for empathy, creativity, and strategic thinking - and when a purely algorithmic approach may suffice. We'll also delve deeper into how to combine the best of both worlds: **humans + AI**.

Before continuing, take a moment to reflect on where you see the greatest "wonder of AI" in your own context. Is it automating a laborious process? Or perhaps providing real-time insights you never thought possible? By identifying these opportunities, you'll be ready to harness AI's potential - and shape it to serve truly human-centered goals.

Key Takeaways

- **Perception**: AI can "see" (image recognition), "read" (text analysis), and "hear" (speech recognition), enhancing tasks from medical diagnostics to global collaboration.
- **Inference**: Predictive models help organizations anticipate needs, detect fraud, and forecast demand, driving efficiency and proactive decision-making.
- **Decision & Action**: Self-driving vehicles, automated trading systems, and advanced robotics use AI to make informed decisions with minimal human intervention.
- **Creative Output**: AI tools assist animators, writers, and designers by generating initial drafts or concepts, freeing them to focus on higher-level creativity and emotional resonance.
- **Collaboration Is Key**: AI's wonders are fully realized when humans guide its efforts, refine its outputs, and infuse ethical considerations and empathy into the final product.

The four areas of AI "wonder" represent practical, exciting directions for innovation. By understanding how AI perceives, infers, decides, and even creates, you lay the groundwork for meaningful, high-impact applications - often far beyond what we once believed machines could do.

CHAPTER 5

When Do We Need Human Compassion?

"AI excels at optimization, but it's the human heart that brings empathy, compassion, and nuanced judgment"

Innovation in AI has led to a spectrum of possible applications - from efficient data-driven processes that require minimal human oversight to complex decisions where empathy and creativity are indispensable. Understanding **which tasks to automate** vs. **which tasks to augment with human compassion** becomes critical for truly successful AI-driven solutions. In this chapter, we explore the *types of AI* in the context of *compassion, creativity, and strategy,* and discuss how to determine the right balance of "human + AI" for different scenarios.

5.1 Defining the Spectrum: Compassion vs. Optimization

One useful way to categorize tasks involves two dimensions:

Compassion Needed vs. Not Needed

- **High Compassion**: Interactions that require empathy, emotional intelligence, or sensitive judgment (e.g., counseling, healthcare, delicate customer service).
- **Low Compassion**: Processes where emotional considerations are minimal or irrelevant (e.g., warehouse inventory checks, data crunching).

Creativity/Strategy vs. Pure Optimization

- **High Creativity/Strategy**: Tasks that call for out-of-the-box thinking, complex problem-solving, or strategic decision-making in uncertain environments.

- **Low Creativity/Strategy**: Well-defined tasks with a clear set of parameters and outcomes (e.g., repetitive assembly, simple classification).

By combining these two axes, we can group tasks into quadrants - identifying when **AI** alone is sufficient, when **human involvement** is essential, and when a **hybrid model** is optimal.

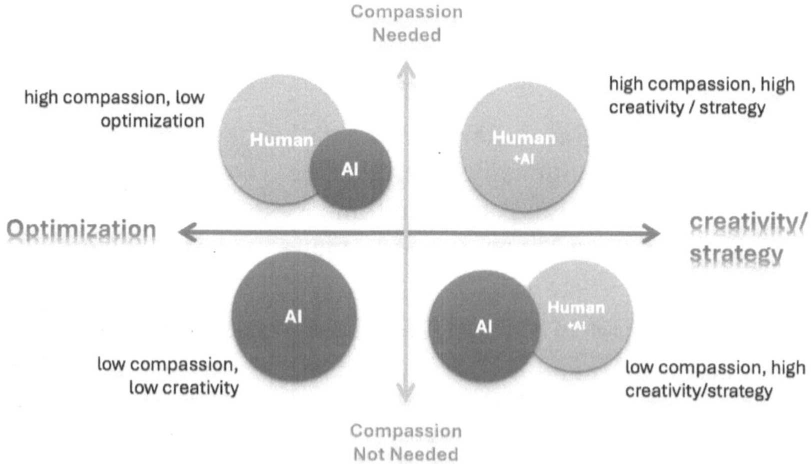

*Figure 7: Analytics is a tool to solve business problems**

5.2 Quadrant Breakdown: Where AI Shines and Where Humans Excel

5.2.1 High Compassion + High Creativity/Strategy

Human Dominant: AI can assist by providing data insights or suggestions, but it's the human who must engage empathetically.

Examples:

- **Therapy and Counseling**: AI could transcribe sessions or analyze speech patterns, but genuine empathy and trust-building come from a human therapist.

**"This structure/shape was developed based on concepts/ideas that were reviewed during an Industry session in the post graduate program in AI for Leaders (UT Austin McCombs / Great Learning)."*

- **Executive Leadership**: Complex decisions about company culture, employee well-being, and strategic pivots demand high emotional intelligence and visionary thinking.

5.2.2 High Compassion + Low Optimization

Human + AI: While compassion is pivotal, some processes can be streamlined with AI.

Examples:

- **Customer Support Escalations**: Chatbots handle routine questions, humans step in for emotionally charged issues.
- **Healthcare Triage**: AI assists in preliminary diagnosis, but the final communication and emotional support require nurses or doctors.

5.2.3 Low Compassion + High Creativity/Strategy

Human + AI: Creativity and strategic thinking often benefit from AI-driven data analysis.

Examples:

- **Product Design**: AI generates rapid prototypes or suggests novel design combinations, while the human designer decides which resonate best with brand and user context.
- **Business Strategy**: AI can forecast market trends; leaders then shape strategic moves that blend data with intuition and domain expertise.

5.2.4 Low Compassion + Low Creativity

AI Dominant: Tasks with clear rules and minimal emotional or creative input can be largely automated.

Examples:

- **Order Processing and Fulfillment**: AI-driven systems handle repetitive tasks like labeling packages or sorting shipments.

- **Basic Data Entry**: Automated workflows extract, verify, and categorize data with minimal human oversight.

5.3 When to Combine Human and AI Efforts

5.3.1 Recognizing Where AI Struggles

AI models can stumble in contexts requiring emotional nuance, complex moral judgment, or situations where the dataset is too small or unrepresentative. Identifying these limitations early ensures humans remain in the loop.

5.3.2 Designing the Handoff

Many processes benefit from a "human-in-the-loop" design, where AI handles 80–90% of the routine work, and humans step in for the final 10–20%. This approach maximizes efficiency while preserving empathy and context-sensitivity.

Practical Tips:

- Set clear rules for when AI flags a task for human review.
- Provide user-facing messaging that clarifies when an interaction transitions from AI to a human agent (e.g., "Transferring you to a specialist now…").

5.3.3 Balancing Costs with Value

Bringing humans into the process usually increases labor costs but might yield better outcomes in critical decisions or high-touch interactions. Conduct a cost-benefit analysis to see whether the **improved user satisfaction or error reduction** justifies the additional resource investment.

5.4 Real-World Examples: Human + AI in Practice

5.4.1 Telehealth Services

- **AI Role**: Analyzes patient intake forms, flags potential emergencies, suggests possible diagnoses.
- **Human Role**: Provides emotional support, interprets nuances of patient history, makes the final call on treatment.
- **Value**: Medical professionals focus on complex cases where empathy and expertise are paramount, while AI handles repetitive triage work.

5.4.2 Marketing Campaigns

- **AI Role**: Predicts customer behavior, segments audiences, automates A/B testing for ad copy.
- **Human Role**: Crafts the brand's emotional message, decides which creative direction aligns with brand identity, builds relationships with high-value customers.
- **Value**: Marketers spend more time on high-level creative strategy and less on repetitive optimizations.

5.4.3 Education and Tutoring

- **AI Role**: Personalizes lesson plans, identifies student weaknesses in real time, tracks progress.
- **Human Role**: Encourages, motivates, and reassures students; tailors instruction to emotional and social contexts.
- **Value**: Students receive targeted support, while teachers free themselves from routine grading and administrative tasks.

5.5 Ethical Implications: Keeping Humans in Control

Automation can be seductive - cutting costs, speeding up processes - but there's a **moral dimension** to offloading decisions to machines, particularly where well-being and dignity are at stake.

- **Accountability**: Who is responsible if an AI-driven recommendation causes harm or distress?
- **Bias and Fairness**: AI might inadvertently discriminate if trained on biased data. Human oversight ensures equitable treatment.
- **Trust and Transparency**: Users should know when they're interacting with AI vs. a human. Clear policies foster trust in AI systems.

5.6 Key Considerations for Selecting AI-Driven vs. Human-Driven Approaches

- **Task Complexity**: Does the job involve multiple variables or changing conditions that a static model might struggle with?
- **Data Availability**: Is there enough clean, relevant data for AI to learn effectively?
- **Emotional Sensitivity**: Does success hinge on empathy, persuasion, or cultural nuances?
- **Risk Tolerance**: Are mistakes high-stakes, possibly harming individuals or reputations? If so, human judgment may need to override AI decisions.
- **Strategic Value**: Will a human perspective offer a strategic advantage or unique insight?

5.7 Looking Ahead

We've now established a framework for determining when AI can stand alone, when it should be guided by human oversight, and when it absolutely **must** be supported by compassion and creativity. In the next chapter, we'll explore **the AI maturity journey** - how organizations progress from being novices (or skeptics) to fully integrating AI in ways that maximize business and societal value.

Key Takeaways

- **Framework for Task Analysis**: Assess tasks by their need for compassion and creativity/strategy vs. pure optimization.
- **Human + AI**: Most real-world scenarios benefit from combining the strengths of both AI and humans, especially in emotionally charged or high-stakes areas.

- **Ethical Dimensions**: Automating sensitive tasks must be approached with caution and clear accountability.
- **Context Matters**: No one-size-fits-all approach. Each organization and process may require a unique balance of human empathy and AI efficiency.
- **Focus on Value**: The ultimate goal is to deliver better outcomes - faster processes, improved customer experiences, or more insightful decisions - while preserving human dignity and creativity.

Striking the perfect balance between human compassion and AI-driven optimization can be a game-changer. It's not just about what tasks get automated; it's about how we deploy AI *responsibly* to enhance human potential and deliver genuinely transformative results.

CHAPTER 6

The AI Maturity Journey

"AI adoption isn't a one-time decision; it's a continuous evolution of strategy, culture, and capability."

Many organizations dream of leveraging AI to drive efficiency, spur innovation, or gain competitive advantage. But few understand that success requires more than a flashy proof of concept. It involves an orchestrated progression - what we call an **AI maturity journey** - through which a company evolves from basic experimentation to fully integrated, enterprise-wide AI deployment.

In this chapter, we outline the common stages of AI maturity (Novice, Ready, Proficient, Advanced), explore the key pillars that shape AI adoption, and provide guidance on how organizations can navigate each phase.

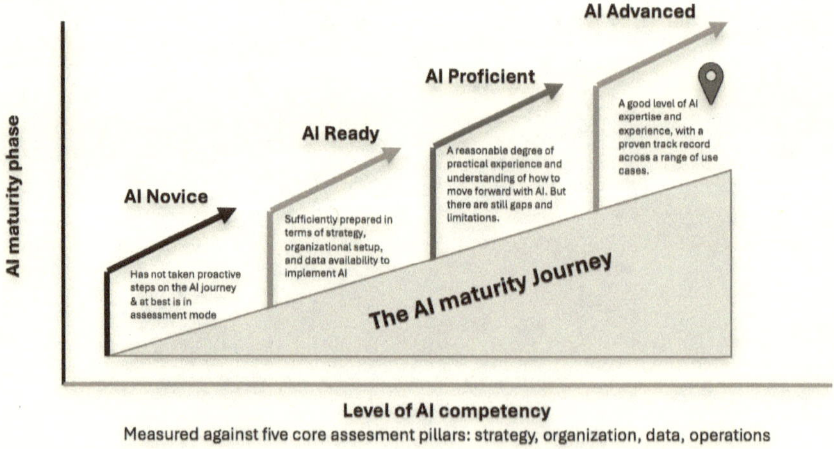

*Figure 8: Stages on the road to AI maturity**

**"This structure/shape was developed based on concepts/ideas that were reviewed during an Industry session in the post graduate program in AI for Leaders (UT Austin McCombs / Great Learning)."*

6.1 The Four Stages of AI Maturity

6.1.1 AI Novice

Characteristics:

- Limited or no formal AI projects underway.
- Leadership may still be skeptical or uncertain about AI's relevance.
- Data and infrastructure are poorly organized, and there's no clear AI strategy in place.

Typical Mindset:

- "Should we even invest in AI?"
- "We don't have enough data or the right people to do this."

Immediate Steps:

- **Awareness & Education**: Train decision-makers on AI fundamentals - use cases, benefits, limitations.
- **Data Audit**: Start understanding the data you have and its quality.
- **Low-Risk Pilots**: Conduct small experiments or POCs (proofs of concept) to showcase AI's potential value.

6.1.2 AI Ready

Characteristics:

- AI curiosity is turning into concrete plans.
- Management has begun allocating resources for AI initiatives.
- Data pipelines and foundational tools (cloud platforms, analytics infrastructure) are in early stages of development.

Typical Mindset:

- "We see AI's potential, but how do we implement it effectively?"
- "We need a strategy that aligns AI projects with business goals."

Immediate Steps:

- **Strategic Alignment**: Identify high-impact business problems that AI could solve (e.g., reducing customer churn, optimizing supply chain).
- **Build a Core Team**: Hire or designate key roles - Data Scientist, Data Engineer, Project Manager - to champion AI projects.
- **Data Governance**: Start standardizing data collection, storage, and cleaning processes to ensure quality and compliance.

6.1.3 AI Proficient

Characteristics:

- The organization has delivered successful AI pilots and is beginning to expand use cases.
- AI knowledge is spreading - business units are aware of AI's capabilities, and specialized teams handle technical execution.
- Data strategy and operational processes are maturing, though there may still be gaps in scaling and cross-functional collaboration.

Typical Mindset:

  - "AI works. Now, how do we make it part of our standard toolbox?"
  - "We need to streamline workflows and governance to handle more complex initiatives."

Immediate Steps:

- **Process Integration**: Incorporate AI outputs into everyday decision-making (e.g., personalized marketing, predictive maintenance).
- **MLOps & Automation**: Automate model deployment, monitoring, and updates for consistent performance across multiple use cases.
- **Talent Development**: Provide ongoing training and development for teams to keep up with AI advancements and best practices.

6.1.4 AI Advanced

Characteristics:

- AI is woven into the fabric of the company's operations and culture.
- Multiple AI models run concurrently across different departments, driving measurable ROI.
- Sophisticated infrastructure, data pipelines, and governance frameworks support continuous innovation.

Typical Mindset:

- "AI is core to our competitive advantage."
- "We must stay at the cutting edge of research and technology to maintain our lead."

Immediate Steps:

- **Scale and Innovate**: Expand AI solutions to new domains, possibly exploring advanced techniques (reinforcement learning, neural-symbolic approaches).
- **Global Collaboration**: Engage in partnerships with research labs, universities, or open-source communities to stay ahead of emerging trends.
- **Ethics & Governance**: Strengthen ethical guidelines and compliance checks, ensuring AI use aligns with societal and regulatory expectations.

6.2 The Five Core Assessment Pillars

Progress through these stages is often measured against five critical pillars. While we've woven these through the above stages, let's explicitly define them here:

6.2.1 Strategy

- **Definition**: Clear vision for how AI will create business value.

- **Key Question**: Are AI initiatives aligned with the organization's strategic goals and performance metrics?

6.2.2 Organization

- **Definition**: Cultural readiness, leadership support, and defined roles for AI.
- **Key Question**: Does leadership champion AI? Are there cross-functional teams dedicated to AI projects?

6.2.3 Data

- **Definition**: Availability, quality, and management of data, including pipelines and governance.
- **Key Question**: Are data sources well-defined, accurate, and scalable?

6.2.4 Operations

- **Definition**: Day-to-day processes and infrastructures that facilitate AI deployment and maintenance (think MLOps, DevOps).
- **Key Question**: Do we have robust systems for deploying, monitoring, and updating AI models?

6.2.5 People & Skills

(sometimes included within "Organization," but important enough to highlight separately)

- **Definition**: Talent and expertise available to design, implement, and scale AI initiatives.
- **Key Question**: Do we have the right mix of data scientists, engineers, analysts, and business experts to support AI?

6.3 Typical Challenges at Each Stage

6.3.1 From Novice to Ready

- **Challenge**: Skepticism or lack of understanding among top management.
- **Overcome By**: Quick-win projects showcasing tangible ROI or improvements in efficiency.

6.3.2 From Ready to Proficient

- **Challenge**: Managing siloed AI projects that lack a unifying strategy or data architecture.
- **Overcome By**: Developing an enterprise-wide AI roadmap, establishing centralized data governance, and creating best practices for model deployment.

6.3.3 From Proficient to Advanced

- **Challenge**: Scaling infrastructure and ensuring consistent performance across multiple models and business units.
- **Overcome By**: Investing in robust MLOps, adopting agile methodologies for AI projects, and fostering cross-functional expertise.

6.4 Assessing Your Organization's Position

Organizations often find themselves straddling more than one stage - perhaps "AI Ready" in one department but still "Novice" in others. A realistic self-assessment can identify inconsistencies and reveal priorities.

Self-Audit Tools: Many consulting firms and tech vendors offer AI readiness assessments.

Key Indicators:

- The frequency of data-driven decisions
- The proportion of processes already automated or augmented by AI

- Leadership's AI vision and budget allocation
- Employee skill levels in data science, ML, and AI engineering

6.5 Practical Tips for Advancing AI Maturity

6.5.1 Develop a Coherent Vision:

- Build consensus around how AI aligns with long-term business strategy.
- Communicate use cases that inspire cross-departmental buy-in.

6.5.2 Start Small, Scale Fast:

- Experiment with pilot projects in a controlled environment.
- Quickly iterate on successful pilots, rolling them out more broadly once they prove value.

6.5.3 Invest in People:

- Train your existing workforce through workshops, online courses, or mentorship programs.
- Recruit or contract specialized talent if necessary - Data Scientists, ML Engineers, MLOps specialists.

6.5.4 Implement Strong Governance:

- Establish data governance policies for data privacy, quality, and compliance (GDPR, CCPA, etc.).
- Set ethical standards and accountability frameworks for AI decision-making.

6.5.5 Leverage Partnerships:

- Collaborate with universities, research labs, or AI startups to stay updated on emerging technologies.
- Join industry consortiums to learn from peers and share best practices.

6.5.6 Continuous Improvement Mindset:

- Integrate agile methodologies to adapt AI solutions in response to changing data and market conditions.
- Use iterative feedback loops, performance tracking, and model retraining to keep AI applications relevant and accurate.

6.6 Looking Ahead

Reaching "AI Advanced" doesn't signal an endpoint - it's simply the stage where AI becomes a driving force in ongoing innovation. As new technologies emerge (think quantum computing, more advanced neural networks, or specialized hardware accelerators), even "AI Advanced" organizations will need to evolve.

In the next chapter, we'll dive into the **Data Science Lifecycle** - a process blueprint that helps teams move from raw data to actionable AI insights. Whether you're an AI Novice or already AI Proficient, **understanding the lifecycle** is crucial for building, evaluating, and continuously improving AI models in a structured, repeatable manner.

Key Takeaways

- **AI Maturity Is a Journey**: Ranging from Novice to Advanced, each stage reflects increasing sophistication in strategy, data handling, and organizational readiness.
- **Five Core Pillars**: Strategy, organization, data, operations, and people/skills must align for successful AI adoption and scaling.
- **Challenges Vary by Stage**: Whether overcoming skepticism, breaking down silos, or scaling infrastructure, each maturity level has distinct hurdles.
- **Structured Growth**: Quick wins build momentum; strong governance, clear strategy, and ongoing skill development sustain progress.
- **Continuous Evolution**: Even advanced AI organizations must adapt to new technologies, data realities, and ethical considerations.

By defining your position on the AI maturity spectrum, you can chart a realistic path forward - investing in the right areas at the right time, rallying stakeholders around shared goals, and building a future-ready enterprise where AI seamlessly powers everyday decisions.

CHAPTER 7

The Data Science Lifecycle (DSLC)

"AI without data is like an engine without fuel. The quality and flow of data determine how far - and how smoothly - your AI can take you."

No AI system can function without data. Yet, data alone is not enough. The real challenge lies in managing the entire cycle - from acquiring raw data to deploying an AI model in production and continually refining it. This **Data Science Lifecycle (DSLC)** provides a framework to tackle these tasks systematically. By understanding each stage, organizations can ensure that **insights are accurate, models are robust,** and **outcomes deliver real business value**.

7.1 Overview of the DSLC Stages

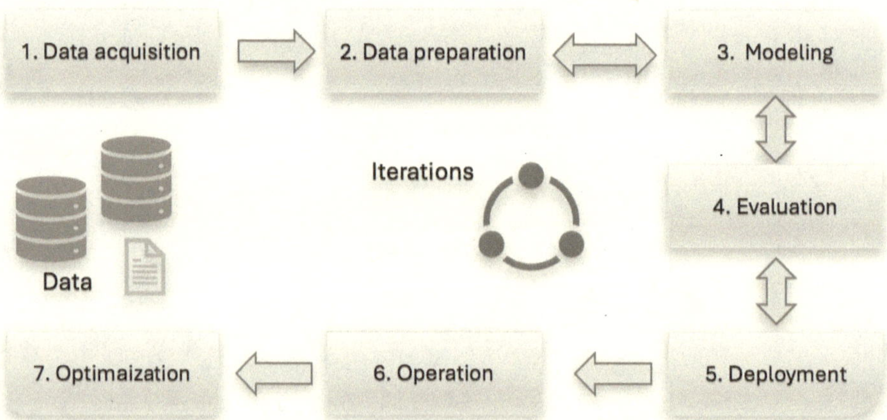

Figure 9: Data Science Lifecycle (DSLC)

Each step connects to the next, creating an iterative process. Let's explore these stages in detail.

7.2 Stage 1: Data Acquisition

"Collect data before you need it." – A common aphorism in data science

7.2.1 Identifying Data Sources

- **Internal Systems**: CRM databases, ERP logs, user-generated content.
- **External Sources**: Public datasets, API feeds (social media, weather, economic indicators).
- **Sensor/IoT Data**: Real-time streams from manufacturing machines, autonomous vehicles, or smart devices.

7.2.2 Quality and Relevance

- **Data Validity**: Are the data points accurate, consistent, and free of corruption?
- **Coverage**: Does the dataset represent all the scenarios or user behaviors you care about?
- **Ethical Considerations**: Are you respecting privacy regulations (GDPR, CCPA) and ethical standards when acquiring data?

Key Outcomes

- A **raw dataset** (structured or unstructured) stored securely.
- Initial insights into potential biases, missing values, or ethical red flags.

7.3 Stage 2: Data Preparation

"80% of a data scientist's work is cleaning the data - the rest is complaining about cleaning the data." – Jokingly shared within data science circles

7.3.1 Data Cleaning

- **Handling Missing Values**: Techniques include imputation, deletion, or modeling missing data.

- **Removing Duplicates**: Ensures records are unique to avoid skewed results.
- **Addressing Outliers**: Deciding whether outliers are valid data points or anomalies to remove.

7.3.2 Feature Engineering

- **Transformation**: Converting raw data into meaningful features (e.g., extracting week-of-year from a timestamp).
- **Encoding**: Turning categorical variables (like "city name") into numeric representations for machine learning models.
- **Dimensionality Reduction**: PCA or autoencoders can simplify datasets with many features, reducing noise and overfitting.

7.3.3 Data Splitting

- **Training, Validation, Test Sets**: Ensures models learn patterns effectively, with separate datasets to tune hyperparameters (validation) and measure final performance (test).

7.3.4 Key Outcomes

- A **clean, structured dataset** where key features are defined.
- Clear data splits for modeling and evaluation.

7.4 Stage 3: Modeling

"All models are wrong, but some are useful." – George E. P. Box (statistician)

7.4.1 Selecting Algorithms

The choice depends on the **problem type** (classification, regression, clustering) and **data characteristics** (size, structure):

- **Classical ML** (Decision Trees, Random Forests, XGBoost) vs.
- **Deep Learning** (Convolutional Neural Networks, Recurrent Neural Networks) vs.

- **Reinforcement Learning** (Q-learning, policy gradients) in dynamic or interactive environments.

7.4.2 Hyperparameter Tuning

- **Grid Search / Random Search**: Systematically explore parameter combinations.
- **Bayesian Optimization**: Iteratively refines choices based on past performance, often more efficient.

7.4.3 Model Training

- **Resource Allocation**: Use GPUs for deep learning if large-scale computations are needed.
- **Time vs. Accuracy Trade-offs**: Some models train quickly but may not achieve high accuracy, while complex models (like large neural networks) can require significant time and resources.

7.4.4 Key Outcomes

- A trained **model** with a set of **hyperparameters** that produce good performance on the training dataset.

7.5 Stage 4: Evaluation

"Validation data is your friend - it keeps you honest."

7.5.1 Metrics and KPIs

- **Classification**: Accuracy, Precision, Recall, F1-Score, ROC-AUC.
- **Regression**: RMSE, MAE, R-squared.
- **Clustering/Segmentation**: Silhouette score, Davies-Bouldin index.
- **Business KPIs**: Customer churn rate, conversion rate lift, cost savings.

7.5.2 Model Validation

- **Hold-Out Validation**: Using a separate validation set to tweak hyperparameters.
- **Cross-Validation**: K-fold approach to maximize data usage for both training and validation.
- **Real-World Testing**: Pilot deployments or shadow runs to gauge performance in live conditions.

7.5.3 Bias and Fairness Checks

- **Demographic Parity**: Are predictions fair across different demographic groups?
- **Explainability**: Tools like SHAP or LIME can provide insights into which features influence predictions.

7.5.4 Key Outcomes

- A clear sense of **model performance**, both technically and from a business perspective.
- Identification of any **ethical or fairness issues** before deployment.

7.6 Stage 5: Deployment

"A model not in production is just an expensive science project."

7.6.1 Deployment Strategies

- **Batch Processing**: Periodically run the model on incoming data (e.g., once a day).
- **Real-Time Inference**: APIs or microservices provide on-demand predictions with minimal latency.
- **Edge Deployment**: AI models run on local devices for immediate results (e.g., self-driving cars, IoT sensors).

7.6.2 MLOps Practices

- **Continuous Integration/Continuous Deployment (CI/CD)**: Automate the build, testing, and release of ML pipelines.
- **Version Control for Models**: Tag models with version numbers or commit hashes to track changes over time.
- **Monitoring and Logging**: Keep track of model performance, data drift, and system usage in real time.

7.6.3 Key Outcomes

- **Live AI system** interacting with users or processes.
- Documentation and versioning that streamline future updates.

7.7 Stage 6: Operation

"Production is just the beginning of a model's life - not the end."

7.7.1 Monitoring Model Health

- **Data Drift**: The input data changes over time (e.g., new consumer behaviors), causing model performance to degrade.
- **Model Drift**: Model predictions worsen because the real world no longer matches the training environment.
- **Alert Systems**: Automatic notifications if error rates exceed thresholds or drift is detected.

7.7.2 User Feedback Loop

- **Human Oversight**: Feedback from end-users can pinpoint where the model excels or fails.
- **Retraining Triggers**: Schedule model retraining or fine-tuning based on performance degradation or new data availability.

7.7.3 Key Outcomes

- Ongoing **model maintenance** with an established feedback mechanism.

- Insights into **real-world behavior** and how the model adapts over time.

7.8 Stage 7: Optimization

"The best model today might be outdated tomorrow - data and objectives constantly evolve."

7.8.1 Continuous Improvement

- **New Data Integration**: Incorporate recent data to reflect changing trends and patterns.
- **Hyperparameter Tuning Cycles**: Revisit parameter choices as data grows or changes.
- **Explore Advanced Techniques**: Consider switching from classical ML to deep learning, or from a single model to an ensemble.

7.8.2 Efficiency Gains

- **Resource Optimization**: Prune or compress large models for faster inference, cheaper cloud costs, or lower power consumption.
- **Scalability**: Migrate to more robust architectures (e.g., distributed computing) to handle surges in demand.

7.8.3 Business Alignment

- **Refine KPIs**: As business goals evolve, re-align your AI metrics.
- **Cross-Functional Feedback**: Engage various departments (sales, marketing, operations) to ensure the AI remains strategically relevant.

7.9 Why the DSLC Is Iterative

The Data Science Lifecycle is not strictly linear; **each stage influences and refines the other**. For instance, model evaluation might reveal data quality issues, prompting a return to the data preparation phase. Continuous iteration ensures that AI systems remain agile, up-to-date, and aligned with ever-changing business and societal needs.

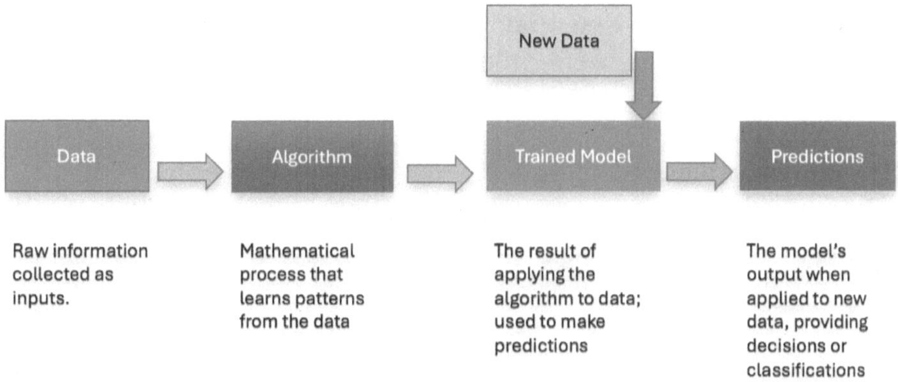

Figure 10: AI Workflow: From Data to Predictions

7.10 Looking Ahead

Mastering the DSLC helps organizations develop AI projects that are not only successful **at launch** but remain valuable **throughout their operational life**. However, the journey from raw data to fully integrated AI is rarely smooth - it requires a **dedicated AI team** and effective collaboration among various stakeholders.

In the next chapter, we'll outline the **minimal AI team structure**, detailing **who does what** and **why each role matters**. From data engineers to business analysts, understanding these roles is crucial to accelerating and sustaining your AI initiatives.

Key Takeaways

- **DSLC Provides Structure**: A systematic approach to data acquisition, cleaning, modeling, deployment, and ongoing maintenance.
- **Data Quality Is King**: Good outcomes hinge on robust data pipelines and proper governance.
- **Evaluation and Monitoring**: Continual checks ensure models remain accurate, fair, and aligned with business goals.
- **Deployment ≠ End**: Real-world shifts in data or objectives demand ongoing monitoring, retraining, and optimization.

- **Collaboration Is Essential**: Successful lifecycle execution involves data scientists, engineers, product owners, and executives each playing complementary roles.

By following the DSLC, you set the stage for **scalable, resilient AI solutions** that can adapt over time, ultimately delivering sustained value instead of a one-off result.

CHAPTER 8

Building an AI Team

"AI is a team sport - no single individual can master data engineering, modeling, business strategy, and deployment all at once."

Having established the Data Science Lifecycle (DSLC), it's clear that creating and maintaining AI solutions is an inherently collaborative process. A single "AI expert" can't single-handedly manage data pipelines, build models, and align everything with strategic business goals. Instead, organizations need a cross-functional team, each member bringing specialized skills.

This chapter outlines the *minimal set of roles* crucial for any AI initiative, highlights how they collaborate, and provides insights on building or upskilling your AI workforce.

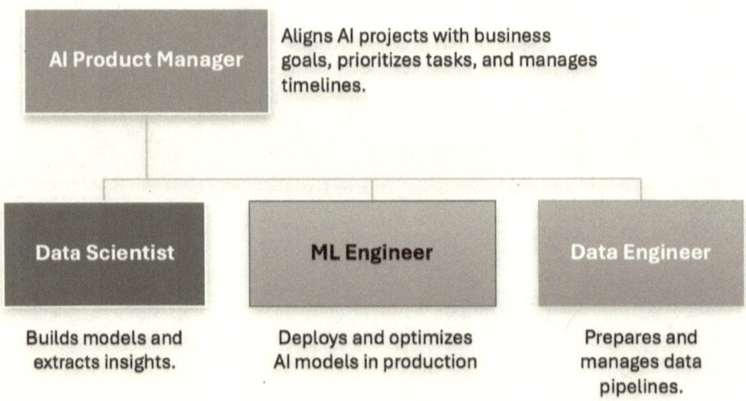

Figure 11: Minimal AI team

8.1 Why Cross-Functional Teams Matter

- **Diverse Perspectives**: Data scientists excel at modeling, but they need domain experts to interpret results. Meanwhile, software engineers ensure robust, scalable deployments.
- **Shared Accountability**: No single role "owns" AI. By distributing responsibilities, organizations avoid bottlenecks and share risk.
- **Faster Iteration**: When each stage of the DSLC has a designated expert, teams can iterate efficiently, reducing time-to-market for AI solutions.

8.2 Core Roles in the Minimal AI Team

8.2.1 Business Lead or Product Owner

Primary Focus: Align AI projects with business strategy.

- **Key Responsibilities:**
    - Identify high-impact use cases that advance organizational goals.
    - Define success metrics and key performance indicators (KPIs).
    - Communicate value propositions to stakeholders and champion AI adoption.
- **Ideal Background**: A blend of domain expertise (finance, marketing, healthcare, etc.) and enough AI knowledge to communicate effectively with technical teams.

8.2.2 Data Engineer

Primary Focus: Ensure reliable data pipelines and infrastructure.

- **Key Responsibilities:**
    - Ingest, transform, and store data efficiently (ETL or ELT processes).
    - Maintain data warehouses, lakes, or real-time streaming systems.
    - Implement security and compliance measures.

- **Ideal Background**: Proficiency in SQL/NoSQL databases, cloud services (AWS, Azure, GCP), and pipeline automation tools (e.g., Airflow, Spark).

8.2.3 Data Scientist / ML Engineer

Primary Focus: Model-building, experimentation, and algorithm design.

- Key Responsibilities:
  - Explore datasets to extract insights (statistical analysis, feature engineering).
  - Train, tune, and evaluate machine learning or deep learning models.
  - Collaborate with data engineers for data access and with MLOps for deployment.
- **Ideal Background**: Strong math/statistics foundation, programming skills (Python, R), familiarity with ML frameworks (TensorFlow, PyTorch, Scikit-learn).

8.2.4 MLOps / DevOps Engineer

Primary Focus: Bridge development and production for ML models.

- Key Responsibilities:
  - Containerize models (Docker, Kubernetes) and manage versioning.
  - Automate continuous integration/continuous deployment (CI/CD) for AI workflows.
  - Monitor model performance in production, detecting data or model drift.
- **Ideal Background**: Software engineering and DevOps practices, cloud infrastructure orchestration, familiarity with ML model serving (e.g., TensorFlow Serving, TorchServe).

8.2.5 Analyst / Data Translator

Primary Focus: Serve as a conduit between the technical and non-technical stakeholders.

- Key Responsibilities:
  - Clarify requirements from business teams, ensuring data scientists understand the problem context.
  - Interpret model results for executives, bridging technical complexity with practical insights.
  - Provide feedback loops from end-users to the data science team for continuous improvement.
- **Ideal Background**: Strong communication skills, a basic understanding of statistics and business processes, an aptitude for storytelling with data.

8.3 Optional (But Valuable) Roles

8.3.1 UI/UX Designer

- **Contribution**: Ensures AI-driven applications are intuitive, user-friendly, and accessible.
- **Example**: Designing dashboards for real-time analytics or streamlined front-end interfaces for end-users interacting with AI predictions.

8.3.2 Subject Matter Experts (SMEs)

- **Contribution**: Deep domain knowledge (e.g., medical, financial, retail).
- **Example**: Advising on regulatory constraints, identifying relevant features in specialized datasets, validating model outputs for domain-specific accuracy.

8.3.3 AI/ML Researcher

- **Contribution**: Focuses on pushing the boundaries of existing algorithms or adapting cutting-edge research to organizational use cases.
- **Example**: Experimenting with novel neural network architectures, reinforcement learning strategies, or advanced NLP models.

8.4 Collaboration Across the DSLC

8.4.1 Data Acquisition & Preparation

- Data Engineer ensures raw data is accessible, clean, and well-structured.
- Data Scientist suggests how to transform data into usable formats (feature engineering).
- Analyst or SMEs guide which data variables are most relevant to the business case.

8.4.2 Modeling & Evaluation

- Data Scientist / ML Engineer designs experiments and selects algorithms.
- MLOps helps to automate model training, testing, and environment replication.
- Business Lead/Analyst defines metrics that map back to ROI or customer satisfaction.

8.4.3 Deployment & Operation

- MLOps/DevOps manages environment provisioning, containerization, and monitoring for production.
- Data Scientist remains on standby for model retraining, iteration, or feature updates.
- Analyst gathers user feedback, ensuring the solution meets real-world needs.

8.4.4 Optimization & Continuous Improvement

- Business Lead re-evaluates the strategic fit of the model; suggests new features or additional use cases.
- Data Engineer incorporates fresh data sources if needed.
- All roles collaborate to refine or pivot the solution as the market, data, or organizational priorities evolve.

8.5 Building or Upskilling Your Team

8.5.1 Hiring Strategies

- **Interdisciplinary Focus**: Recruit individuals who thrive in cross-functional settings, not just in a single silo of expertise.
- **Assess Cultural Fit**: AI initiatives require a culture of experimentation, so look for team members comfortable with iteration and ambiguity.
- **Leverage Outsourcing or Consulting**: Early on, it might be more efficient to bring in external experts for specialized tasks - especially if you're an "AI Novice" organization.

8.5.2 Internal Upskilling

- **In-House Workshops**: Offer training sessions on data science basics, coding languages like Python, or tools like SQL and Spark.
- **Mentorship Programs**: Pair junior data analysts with senior data scientists to accelerate learning.
- **Online Courses and Certifications**: Encourage continuous learning through platforms like Coursera, edX, or vendor-specific training (AWS, GCP, Azure).

8.6 Common Pitfalls and How to Avoid Them

Overreliance on a Single "Rockstar"

- **Risk**: Burnout, bottlenecks, and knowledge silo.
- **Solution**: Encourage knowledge sharing, team-based projects, and clear documentation.

Mismatch Between Roles and Expectations

- **Risk**: Data scientists might spend all their time fixing pipelines rather than building models; or business leads might assign impossible deadlines without understanding data complexities.
- **Solution**: Clearly define role responsibilities and maintain open communication channels.

Lack of Executive Sponsorship

- **Risk**: AI projects stall or get deprioritized without budget and leadership support.
- **Solution**: Secure stakeholder buy-in early, emphasize ROI and strategic relevance.

Ignoring Soft Skills

- **Risk**: Even the best technical solutions can fail if teams can't communicate or align with business units.
- **Solution**: Develop interpersonal, presentation, and negotiation skills within the AI team.

8.7 Looking Ahead

Having the *right* team is just as essential as following the *right* process. In the next chapter, we'll shift from the internal mechanics of AI teams to broader considerations of **ethical AI** - exploring how bias, privacy, transparency, and accountability must guide our AI deployments. Even the most skilled team can encounter pitfalls if they neglect the social and ethical dimensions of AI.

Key Takeaways

- **Collaboration Is Crucial**: AI success depends on a coalition of specialized roles - business, data, engineering, operations, and analysis all converging.
- **Minimal AI Team, Maximum Impact**: Even a lean setup needs at least a Business Lead, Data Engineer, Data Scientist, MLOps Engineer, and Analyst to cover the DSLC.
- **Beyond Technical Skills**: Soft skills like communication, empathy, and adaptability are integral to aligning AI projects with real-world needs.
- **Upskilling and Culture**: Continual learning, mentorship, and a culture of experimentation ensure the team stays current and motivated.
- **Evolving Structure**: As the organization's AI maturity grows, so might the team, adding specialists (UI/UX, AI researchers, SMEs) to tackle advanced challenges.

With the right people, processes, and leadership support, your organization can build AI solutions that are both innovative *and* aligned with strategic objectives - laying a solid foundation for responsible, high-impact AI development.

CHAPTER 9

Building Trust and Accountability

"The goal is not just to build powerful AI systems, but to build them in ways that are fair, transparent, and conducive to the well-being of individuals and society."

As AI expands into every facet of our lives - from social media algorithms that shape our newsfeeds, to healthcare diagnostics that can save lives - *ethical considerations* become paramount. Building AI responsibly means going beyond technical prowess and efficiency; it requires accountability, transparency, fairness, and respect for privacy. In this chapter, we will explore the **ethical dimensions** of AI, examine **key concerns** such as bias and privacy, and outline **practical strategies** for maintaining trust and accountability.

9.1 Why Ethical AI Matters

9.1.1 Societal Impact

AI systems can inadvertently **perpetuate inequalities** or harm marginalized communities if they rely on biased data or opaque algorithms. For example, a job screening AI trained on historical hiring data might favor certain demographic groups over others.

9.1.2 Legal and Regulatory Pressures

Governments worldwide are implementing laws and frameworks (GDPR in the EU, CCPA in California) that dictate how organizations must handle data and ensure user protection. Non-compliance can lead to substantial fines and reputational damage.

9.1.3 Long-Term Business Sustainability

Ethical lapses - like leaked personal data or discriminatory AI decisions - can erode consumer trust and loyalty. Conversely, a track record of responsible AI use can become a unique selling point.

9.2 Key Concerns in Ethical AI

9.2.1 Bias

Definition: Bias arises when an AI system produces systematically prejudiced results, often due to skewed training data or flawed modeling assumptions.

Examples:

- Facial recognition that performs poorly on darker skin tones.
- Lending algorithms that disqualify applicants from certain zip codes or economic backgrounds.

Mitigation Strategies:

- Diverse **Training Data**: Seek balanced datasets across gender, ethnicity, age, and more.
- **Bias Audits**: Regularly test algorithms on "protected classes" to detect disparate impacts.
- **Algorithmic Fairness Techniques**: Use frameworks like AIF360 (IBM) or Fairlearn (Microsoft) to measure and mitigate bias.

9.2.2 Privacy

Definition: Ensuring personal data is not misused or exposed without consent.

Regulatory Requirements:

- GDPR mandates data minimization and the "right to be forgotten."
- CCPA grants Californian residents control over personal data collection and usage.

Mitigation Strategies:

- **Data Anonymization/Pseudonymization**: Remove or replace identifying fields whenever possible.
- **Consent Management**: Provide clear opt-in/opt-out mechanisms; respect user choices throughout the data lifecycle.
- **Secure Storage**: Encrypt data at rest and in transit, implement strict access controls.

9.2.3 Transparency

Definition: Users and stakeholders need to understand how and why AI makes certain decisions.

Benefits:

- Builds trust by clarifying the model's logic or data inputs.
- Helps organizations identify and fix errors faster.

Techniques:

- **Explainable AI (XAI)**: Leverage tools (e.g., LIME, SHAP) to show which features most influenced a prediction.
- **Model Documentation**: Maintain "datasheets" for datasets and "model cards" that describe intended use, performance metrics, and known limitations.

9.2.4 Accountability

Definition: Establishing clear responsibility for AI outcomes - both successes and failures.

Challenges:

- Shared responsibility across data providers, developers, and end-users.
- Black-box models can make it difficult to pinpoint blame or cause.

Solutions:

- **Governance Structures**: Define processes for auditing AI decisions, responding to complaints, and rolling back flawed deployments.
- **Human-in-the-Loop**: Require human review for high-stakes decisions (e.g., medical diagnoses, legal judgments).

9.3 Ethical Frameworks and Best Practices

9.3.1 Organizational Policies

- **Code of Conduct**: Outline acceptable AI use, data sharing protocols, and escalation procedures for ethical concerns.
- **Ethics Committees**: Form cross-functional committees (including legal, technical, and community representatives) to evaluate AI projects and resolve ethical dilemmas.

9.3.2 Governance and Oversight

- **Responsible AI Offices**: Some large organizations create dedicated units to oversee AI ethics, model risk management, and compliance.
- **Periodic Ethical Reviews**: Regular intervals to assess the AI systems' impact, data handling, and alignment with the latest regulations or ethical guidelines.

9.3.3 Stakeholder Engagement

- **User Feedback**: Encourage feedback loops where end-users can question or appeal AI decisions.
- **Community Consultation**: Involve external stakeholders, advocacy groups, or domain experts when AI systems could significantly affect public interests.

9.4 Real-World Examples of Ethical AI in Action

9.4.1 Healthcare: AI-Assisted Diagnostics

- **Ethical Consideration**: Potential bias in training data from specific demographics, risk of misdiagnosis.
- **Solution**: Ongoing audits to ensure model accuracy across diverse patient populations, regulatory compliance, and a "doctor-in-the-loop" final decision.

9.4.2 Recruitment and HR Tools

- **Ethical Consideration**: Algorithmic discrimination against certain groups based on historically biased hiring data.
- **Solution**: Use fairness metrics to evaluate HR AI models, integrate anonymized resume review processes, and provide candidates with recourse to challenge decisions.

9.4.3 Credit Scoring

- **Ethical Consideration**: Potentially higher loan rejection rates for certain neighborhoods or socioeconomic groups.
- **Solution**: Deploy fairness algorithms, regularly retrain models with diverse datasets, and offer transparency reports on how credit scores are calculated.

9.5 Practical Steps for Implementing Ethical AI

9.5.1 Start Early

Incorporate ethical guidelines in the project design phase - don't treat it as an afterthought.

9.5.2 Embed Checks Throughout the DSLC

Check for bias, privacy compliance, and transparency at each data science lifecycle stage - from data acquisition to deployment and monitoring.

9.5.3 Educate Your Team

Conduct ethics training so data scientists, engineers, and business stakeholders share a baseline understanding of the risks and responsibilities.

9.5.4 Document Decisions

Maintain a paper trail of design choices, data provenance, and reasoning for key model decisions to facilitate audits and accountability.

9.5.5 Plan for Failures

Anticipate errors or unexpected outcomes; define a rollback mechanism and crisis communication plan if an AI system behaves harmfully or incorrectly.

9.6 Looking Ahead

Ethical AI isn't just a "nice-to-have" - it's a fundamental pillar of sustainable AI adoption. As organizations mature in their AI capabilities, **governance structures** and **ethical reviews** become as essential as technical excellence.

In the upcoming chapters, we'll delve deeper into **practical case studies** of AI at work, showcase how some organizations have successfully blended technology and ethics, and explore how they scale these solutions for long-term impact. Finally, we'll consider the **future landscape** of AI - emerging trends, potential pitfalls, and how to remain both innovative *and* responsible in a rapidly evolving field.

Key Takeaways

- **Ethics Are Non-Negotiable**: Bias, privacy, transparency, and accountability are core concerns, not afterthoughts.
- **Legal Compliance and Beyond**: Regulations like GDPR/CCPA set minimum standards, but forward-thinking organizations move beyond mere compliance to build trust.

- **Bias Isn't Always Obvious**: Continuous monitoring and fairness audits help spot hidden biases.
- **Human Oversight Matters**: Rely on domain experts and structured governance to keep AI decision-making aligned with societal values.
- **Build a Culture of Responsibility**: Ethical AI is less about a single tool or policy and more about an organizational mindset of accountability and respect.

By treating **ethical considerations** as integral to AI development, you safeguard your organization against reputational, legal, and societal risks - ultimately fostering an environment where AI can thrive for the benefit of everyone.

CHAPTER 10

Bridging Business, Math, Data, and Tech

"Real AI breakthroughs occur at the intersection of domain knowledge, robust data strategies, mathematical insight, and technical execution."

Now that we've explored **ethical considerations** and the essential mechanics of AI development - from data pipelines to team structures - it's time to address a broader challenge: *How do we align AI efforts with core business objectives while juggling the complexities of math, data, and technology?*

This chapter delves into **cross-functional alignment**, ensuring that AI initiatives not only succeed on the technical front but also drive meaningful impact for the organization as a whole.

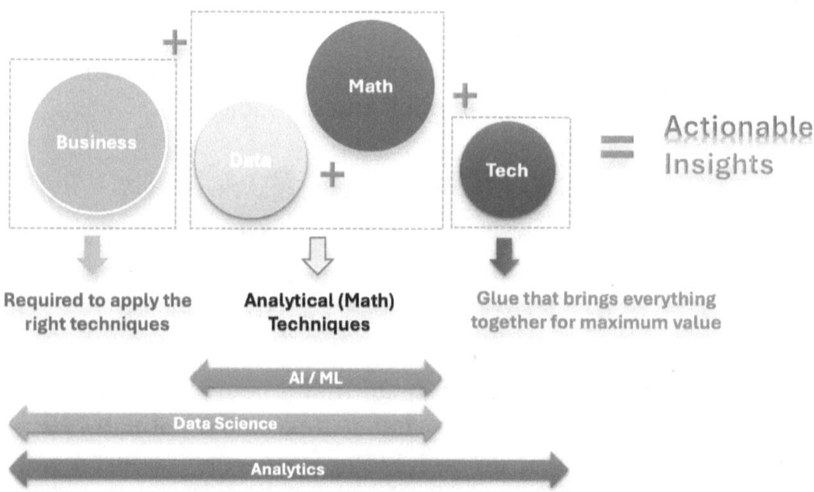

*Figure 12: Analytics is a tool to solve business problems**

**"This structure/shape was developed based on concepts/ideas that were reviewed during an Industry session in the post graduate program in AI for Leaders (UT Austin McCombs / Great Learning)."*

10.1 Why Cross-Disciplinary Collaboration Is Vital

Holistic Problem-Solving:

- Purely technical teams might build state-of-the-art models that lack real business value.
- Conversely, business-focused teams may underestimate the complexity of data and modeling.
- Collaboration ensures the final solution aligns with both user needs and feasibility constraints.

Risk Mitigation:

- A well-rounded team spots pitfalls early - from flawed assumptions in data to misaligned project goals.
- Diverse expertise ensures robust solutions that can adapt when business or technical conditions change.

Efficiency and Momentum:

- Siloed teams often rework tasks or clash over priorities.
- Unified efforts - where business owners, data scientists, and engineers coordinate - keep projects on track and on budget.

10.2 Translating Business Questions into AI Problems

10.2.1 Defining the Business Challenge

- **Concrete Goals**: Identify a quantifiable outcome (e.g., reducing customer churn by 15%, increasing average order value by 10%).
- **Relevant Metrics**: Decide on KPIs upfront - like net promoter score (NPS), revenue growth, or operational efficiency gains.

10.2.2 Assessing Data Readiness

- **Availability**: Do we have the necessary data - user behavior logs, product details, operational metrics?

- **Quality**: Is the data accurate, timely, and representative of all user segments?
- **Ethical/Regulatory Constraints**: Does collecting or using this data align with privacy laws and internal governance policies?

10.2.3 Framing the Problem

- **Classification**: Predict which customers are likely to churn.
- **Regression**: Forecast demand or revenue over a given time horizon.
- **Recommendation**: Suggest personalized products or content.
- **Clustering**: Segment customers or inventory into distinct groups for targeted strategies.

10.3 The Four Pillars of Cross-Functional Success

10.3.1 Business

- **Role**: Set the vision, define success, measure ROI.
- **Key Contribution**: Domain knowledge - understanding the market, competitors, and user needs.
- **Intersection Point**: Collaborates with data translators and data scientists to refine problem statements and validate solutions.

10.3.2 Math (Analytics & Modeling)

- **Role**: Provide the analytical depth - choosing algorithms, interpreting model outcomes, and ensuring statistical validity.
- **Key Contribution**: Transform raw data into predictive or prescriptive insights.
- **Intersection Point**: Works with data engineering to get well-prepared data, and partners with business leads to align model metrics with KPIs.

10.3.3 Data

- **Role**: Manage pipelines, architecture, and governance - ensuring data is clean, accessible, and compliant with regulations.

- **Key Contribution**: Without solid data, AI is prone to poor performance or bias.
- **Intersection Point**: Aligns with both business (to understand which data is relevant) and math teams (to supply the necessary data for modeling).

10.3.4 Technology (Engineering & Operations)

- **Role**: Ensure the technical stack can support model deployment, scalability, and real-time operations.
- **Key Contribution**: Build and maintain the systems that bring AI insights to end-users - e.g., mobile apps, dashboards, or APIs.
- **Intersection Point**: Works closely with the data team on infrastructure and with the math team on model integration (MLOps).

10.4 Strategies to Foster Collaboration

10.4.1 Cross-Functional Task Forces

- **Small, Agile Teams**: Create squads that include at least one member from business, data, math, and tech.
- **Synchronized Goals**: Align everyone on a common success metric (e.g., improve recommendation quality by 20%).
- **Frequent Check-Ins**: Short daily or weekly stand-ups keep communication flowing.

10.4.2 Shared Language and Documentation

- **Glossaries**: Compile a common vocabulary - defining both business terms (LTV, ROI) and technical terms (RMSE, precision, recall).
- **Model Cards and Data Sheets**: Document assumptions, intended use, and limitations for each dataset and model to ensure everyone understands constraints and goals.

10.4.3 Governance Frameworks

- **Steering Committees**: Executive sponsors and domain leaders meet periodically to evaluate AI progress, identify bottlenecks, and re-prioritize projects.
- **Project Charters**: Each AI initiative has a clear scope, milestones, and responsibilities, signed off by all relevant stakeholders.

10.5 Overcoming Common Collaboration Challenges

10.5.1 Misaligned Incentives

- **Issue**: Data teams aim for technical perfection; business teams want quick wins.
- **Solution**: Define success metrics that balance speed, quality, and ROI.

10.5.2 Communication Gaps

- **Issue**: Data scientists speak in terms of "F1 scores" or "AUC," while business leaders focus on revenue or user satisfaction.
- **Solution**: Train data translators or analysts to act as liaisons. Encourage frequent "demo days" where the technical teams showcase progress in clear, tangible terms.

10.5.3 Resource Constraints

- **Issue**: Overworked engineering teams might deprioritize AI pipelines in favor of core system maintenance.
- **Solution**: Secure dedicated budgets and resources for AI projects, track ROI to justify continued investment.

10.5.4 Siloed Data

- **Issue**: Different departments keep separate databases or have conflicting data definitions.

- **Solution**: Implement a unified data governance policy, standardize data definitions, and create centralized or federated data infrastructure.

10.6 Real-World Example: AI-Powered Demand Forecasting

Business Challenge:

- A retailer wants to predict monthly sales to optimize inventory.

Data:

- Historical sales, seasonality indicators, promotional calendars, external factors (weather, economic data).

Math:

- Time-series forecasting models (ARIMA, Prophet, or an LSTM-based neural network).

Technology:

- Data pipelines ingest daily sales updates from POS systems.
- MLOps automates model retraining each month, deploying a new forecasting API.

Cross-Functional Alignment:

- Business: Defines the target (reduce out-of-stock incidents by 30%), sets budget for data engineering improvements.
- **Math**: Selects and tunes the model, ensures the final forecast aligns with business cycles (e.g., weekly vs. monthly).
- **Data**: Maintains a high-quality dataset from multiple store locations and external sources.
- **Technology**: Integrates the forecasting API into the retailer's inventory management system, so it can trigger automated purchase orders.

Outcome: Inventory shortages and overstocks decrease, boosting revenue and enhancing the customer experience. The project's success is driven by aligning **business needs**, **analytical rigor**, **clean data**, and **robust technical infrastructure**.

10.7 Looking Ahead

When business objectives drive AI initiatives - and math, data, and technology teams collaborate effectively - organizations can unlock AI's full potential. This synergy enables faster innovation, reduced risks, and solutions that genuinely move the needle.

In the next chapter, we'll bring these concepts to life through **practical case studies** spanning various industries. We'll see how businesses - from startups to global enterprises - implement AI solutions, address pitfalls, and measure success, illustrating each phase of the AI journey in action.

Key Takeaways

- **Cross-Functional Alignment Is Essential**: Successful AI projects harmonize business strategy, mathematical rigor, data integrity, and technological robustness.
- **Translate Business Needs into AI Goals**: Start with the ROI or key objectives; then map out the data and model requirements.
- **Four Core Pillars**: Each discipline - business, math, data, and tech - adds a unique lens, ensuring well-rounded solutions.
- **Collaboration Tactics**: Agile squads, common glossaries, steering committees, and robust documentation keep teams in sync.
- **Unified Purpose**: When everyone works toward the same metrics and outcomes, AI becomes a strategic lever for transformative growth.

By bridging the gaps between these domains, AI initiatives cease to be isolated tech experiments, evolving instead into integrated solutions that deliver lasting competitive advantage and tangible value.

CHAPTER 11

Practical Case Studies

"The most convincing way to demonstrate AI's value is through real-world examples - where models meet live data, solve tangible problems, and drive measurable impact."

We've covered AI fundamentals, ethical considerations, and the cross-functional collaboration needed to build effective AI solutions. Now it's time to **see these principles in action.** In this chapter, we explore several **practical case studies** from diverse industries - healthcare, retail, finance, and manufacturing - to illustrate how organizations transition from **vision** to **full-scale AI deployment**.

11.1 Healthcare: AI-Assisted Medical Diagnostics

11.1.1 The Challenge

A mid-sized hospital network wants to **reduce diagnostic errors** and **speed up analysis** of chest X-rays to detect early signs of pneumonia. Historically, radiologists have been stretched thin, leading to delays and potential oversight of subtle indicators.

11.1.2 Approach

Data Collection:

- Over 500,000 anonymized chest X-ray images labeled by expert radiologists.
- Additional metadata (age, gender, known medical history) used for context.

Modeling:

- Deployed a Convolutional Neural Network (CNN) trained on a subset of labeled images.
- Validation with a separate set to avoid overfitting and ensure reliable performance metrics.

Deployment and Workflows:

- Integrated the CNN into the hospital's PACS (Picture Archiving and Communication System), so radiologists see **automated highlights** on suspicious areas.
- Radiologists have final review authority, ensuring a **human-in-the-loop** for critical decisions.

Ethical Oversight:

- Committee reviews to ensure patient data privacy, strict anonymization.
- Ongoing bias checks to verify performance consistency across demographic groups.

11.1.3 Outcomes

- **Accuracy**: Reduced missed pneumonia cases by an estimated 25%.
- **Efficiency**: Radiologists saved an average of **2 hours per day**, allowing them to handle more complex cases.
- **Patient Safety**: Earlier detection led to faster treatment, improving patient outcomes and satisfaction.

11.2 Retail: Personalized Recommendations at Scale

11.2.1 The Challenge

An e-commerce company struggles with high customer churn and low engagement. They believe **better product recommendations** could boost repeat purchases and user satisfaction.

11.2.2 Approach

Business Alignment:

- Goal: Increase average order value (AOV) and conversion rates for returning customers by 10%.
- Focus on a segment of high-value products (electronics, home appliances).

Data and Modeling:

- **Data Sources**: Transaction history, browsing behavior, user ratings, item metadata (price, category, brand).
- **Collaborative Filtering**: Basic matrix factorization to find patterns in user-item interactions.
- **Hybrid Model**: Incorporated content-based filtering to recommend products with similar attributes to those users already liked.

Deployment:

- Implemented real-time inference using a cloud-based microservices architecture.
- **A/B Testing**: Rolled out the recommendation engine to a fraction of users initially, measuring lift in conversion rates compared to a control group.

MLOps:

- **Automated** daily retraining to capture new user behaviors and updated inventory.
- Monitoring for data drift (e.g., trending items, seasonal changes).

11.2.3 Outcomes

- **Conversion Lift**: +12% among users exposed to AI-driven recommendations.
- **User Engagement**: Increased time-on-site and repeat visits, contributing to overall revenue growth.

- **Scalable Infrastructure**: The microservices approach allowed the retailer to expand into new markets without overhauling the recommendation system.

11.3 Finance: Automated Fraud Detection

11.3.1 The Challenge

A digital payment platform faces rising transaction fraud, damaging user trust and incurring financial losses. Their existing rule-based system is slow to adapt to new fraud patterns.

11.3.2 Approach

Data Strategy:

- Collected real-time transaction logs (location, device type, transaction amount, user history).
- Historical fraud cases labeled to train **supervised machine learning** models.

Feature Engineering:

- Computed advanced features such as velocity (number of transactions within a short time frame) and geolocation consistency (comparing IP address to registered user address).
- Used **dimensionality reduction** techniques to handle high-volume data from multiple streams.

Machine Learning Pipeline:

- Deployed a **Random Forest** model for baseline detection, combined with an anomaly detection algorithm to flag unusual behavior.
- Continuous retraining every week to incorporate newly confirmed fraud cases.

Real-Time Action:

- Deployed a streaming inference service to assess each transaction within milliseconds.
- Automatically flags suspicious transactions for manual review or requests secondary authentication from the user.

11.3.3 Outcomes

- **Fraud Reduction**: Estimated 40% decrease in fraudulent transactions within the first quarter of deployment.
- **User Trust**: Fewer false positives meant legitimate transactions rarely got flagged incorrectly, maintaining smooth user experience.
- **Adaptive Capability**: The system quickly adapted to emerging fraud patterns, outperforming the old rule-based approach.

11.4 Manufacturing: Predictive Maintenance

11.4.1 The Challenge

A large manufacturing plant grapples with **unplanned downtime** due to equipment failures. Frequent breakdowns disrupt production schedules and lead to significant financial losses.

11.4.2 Approach

Sensor Data Collection:

- Deployed IoT sensors tracking temperature, vibration, RPM, and other metrics.
- Data fed into a central warehouse, then merged with historical maintenance logs.

Predictive Modeling:

- **Time-Series Analysis**: Models like LSTM networks to detect early warning signs of equipment failure.

- **Classification**: Identified high-risk periods (next 7 days) for each machine.

Integration and Alerts:

- Maintenance teams receive automated alerts when a machine is likely to fail soon.
- Scheduled inspections or part replacements to avert downtime.

Continuous Improvement:

- Model performance tracked in real-time, with new sensor data continually improving the predictive accuracy.
- Cross-functional training sessions so operators understand how to respond to alerts.

11.4.3 Outcomes

- **Downtime Decrease**: Reduced unplanned outages by up to 30%, translating directly to cost savings.
- **Inventory Optimization**: Fewer emergency part orders, enabling leaner spare part inventory.
- **Employee Adoption**: Mechanics and operators trusted the system after seeing tangible, reliable alerts, fostering a data-driven culture on the shop floor.

11.5 Key Lessons Across Case Studies

- **Clear Objectives Drive Design**: Each project started with a specific, measurable goal - be it reducing misdiagnoses, boosting sales, cutting fraud, or preventing machine failures.
- **Data Quality Determines Success**: All teams emphasized structured, reliable, and relevant data. Weak or biased datasets undermine the entire effort.
- **Human Oversight Is Crucial**: Even the most sophisticated AI solutions kept humans "in the loop," whether to review fraud cases, interpret medical scans, or finalize strategic decisions.

- **Continuous Feedback & Iteration**: Successful deployments often feature MLOps pipelines that retrain models periodically, incorporate new data, and adapt to changing conditions.
- **Collaboration Leads to Adoption**: The synergy among business stakeholders, data scientists, and operational teams ensured that solutions delivered meaningful, practical outcomes - rather than remaining academic exercises.

11.6 Common Pitfalls to Anticipate

- **Scope Creep**: Trying to solve too many problems at once. Start with a **narrow, high-impact** objective.
- **Model Overfitting**: Especially prevalent when data is noisy or not representative of real-world conditions.
- **Resistance to Change**: Organizational inertia can derail AI adoption. Build trust by showcasing small wins.
- **Ethical Oversights**: Neglecting bias or privacy concerns can lead to reputational damage and regulatory issues.

11.7 Looking Ahead

These case studies demonstrate how AI moves from initial **vision** - a clear, measurable business objective - to **deployment** - a reliable, real-time system used by end-users. Yet, achieving sustainable impact often involves **scaling** these solutions to more teams, different markets, and evolving use cases.

In the next chapter, we'll examine how organizations can **scale and evolve** their AI capabilities - expanding successful pilots into enterprise-wide transformations, and adapting AI initiatives to changing data, technologies, and business landscapes.

Key Takeaways

- Industry-Agnostic Patterns: While details differ, the fundamentals of defining a clear goal, securing quality data, and iterating with a human-in-the-loop apply across sectors.

- **Measurable Outcomes**: Every successful project ties AI results (e.g., reduced downtime, fraud, or churn) back to tangible KPIs or cost savings.
- **Ethics in Action**: Privacy, fairness, and accountability are not theoretical concerns - real projects must bake them into data usage and model deployment processes.
- **MLOps for Sustainability**: Frequent retraining, monitoring, and alerts keep AI models relevant and high-performing.
- **Cultural Integration**: When front-line users (radiologists, mechanics, sales teams) trust and understand AI outputs, adoption and impact skyrocket.

By learning from these diverse success stories - and anticipating common pitfalls - you'll be better equipped to take your AI projects from concept to **concrete, value-generating reality**.

CHAPTER 12

Scaling and Evolving Your AI Capabilities

"An AI solution that stays small, hidden in a single department, misses its true potential. Scaling AI is how you turn niche wins into enterprise-wide transformation."

Having explored **practical case studies** and the foundational elements of AI - people, processes, technology, and ethical considerations - it's time to look at **how to scale** these initiatives. While many organizations achieve *initial AI successes*, fewer manage to make AI a **sustained, driving force** across their enterprise. In this chapter, we examine the strategies, infrastructure, and cultural shifts required to move from *localized pilots* to **ongoing AI evolution**.

12.1 Why Scaling Matters

Enterprise-Wide Impact:

- Single-department AI applications can demonstrate ROI, but broader adoption can *transform entire business models*.
- Scaling AI extends benefits like cost savings, increased revenue, and enhanced customer experiences across multiple teams or geographies.

Continuous Innovation:

- The faster AI solutions can be adapted to new problems, the more flexible and competitive the organization becomes.
- A robust, scalable AI infrastructure helps teams experiment and deploy new models quickly.

Economies of Scale:

- Centralizing data engineering, MLOps, and best practices avoids duplication of effort.
- Larger data volumes from different parts of the organization can improve model accuracy and unlock cross-functional insights.

12.2 Foundations for Scaling AI

12.2.1 Centralized or Federated Data Infrastructure

Data Hubs:

- Many enterprises establish a **data lake** or data warehouse that consolidates information from various departments.
- Ensures **consistent data schemas**, easy access, and streamlined governance.

Federated Approach:

- In some cases, strict data privacy or regulatory requirements necessitate **federated learning**, where models train locally on distributed datasets.
- Ideal for organizations that span multiple jurisdictions with varying rules on data sharing.

12.2.2 Robust MLOps Pipelines

Automated Model Lifecycle:

- Continuous integration/continuous deployment (CI/CD) for machine learning.
- Regularly scheduled retraining and automated monitoring keep models up-to-date with minimal human intervention.

Scalability:

- Infrastructure that can handle **surges** in data volume or computational demands - often via cloud-based solutions like AWS Sagemaker, Google Vertex AI, or Azure ML.
- Containerization (Docker, Kubernetes) for portability and consistent deployment environments.

12.2.3 AI Governance and Standards

Enterprise AI Playbooks:

- Document repeatable processes for data collection, model development, ethical reviews, and deployment.
- Encourage reusability of code modules, data pipelines, and tested machine learning "blueprints."

Compliance and Ethics:

- Scaling AI increases the risk of broad impact.
- Mandatory **bias checks**, **explainability audits**, and **human-in-the-loop** thresholds become essential in high-stakes domains.

12.3 Organizational Structures for Scaled AI

12.3.1 Center of Excellence (CoE)

Description:

- A dedicated hub of AI expertise that supports various departments.
- Provides training, best practices, governance frameworks, and advisory on complex AI initiatives.

Pros:

- Centralized knowledge base, consistent standards, and reduced duplication of effort.

Cons:

- Risk of bottlenecks if the CoE becomes overloaded or if teams remain too dependent on it for execution.

12.3.2 Hub-and-Spoke Model

Description:

- A central AI team (hub) sets the strategy, governance, and architecture, while smaller specialized data science squads (spokes) are embedded in individual business units.

Pros:

- Balances centralized standards with domain-specific expertise.
- Allows each department to tailor AI solutions to their unique needs.

Cons:

- Requires disciplined communication and synchronization between the hub and spokes.

12.3.3 Fully Distributed AI Teams

Description:

- Each department or product team has its own AI capabilities, sharing best practices informally or through cross-functional committees.

Pros:

- Maximal autonomy, immediate alignment with local domain knowledge.

Cons:

- Higher risk of siloed efforts, inconsistent standards, and redundant projects.

12.4 Strategic Roadmap for AI Scaling

Executive Alignment:

- Secure strong sponsorship from C-level executives or board members.
- Clearly articulate the business value of scaling AI - whether it's revenue growth, operational efficiency, or market differentiation.

Pilot-to-Portfolio Transition:

- Evaluate successful pilots for **scalability** and ROI potential.
- Create a **portfolio** of AI projects, each with clear timelines, budgets, and success metrics.

Skill Development:

- Upskill your workforce with **technical training** (data engineering, MLOps) and **soft skills** (communication, change management).
- Consider rotational programs where team members cycle through the AI CoE, learning best practices.

Infrastructure Investments:

- Modernize data architecture to support real-time analytics and high-volume batch processing.
- Adopt DevOps and MLOps tools that automate as many processes (building, testing, deploying) as possible.

Governance & Policy Enforcement:

- Establish an **AI Ethics Board** or designate an **Ethics Officer**.
- Set up routine audits for model performance, data privacy, and regulatory compliance at scale.

Feedback Loops & Continuous Improvement:

- Encourage each department to share lessons learned, code modules, and data pipelines.
- Host internal meetups or "demo days" for teams to showcase AI innovations and receive feedback.

12.5 Handling Growth Challenges

12.5.1 Data Overload

- **Issue**: As more data sources come online, it becomes overwhelming to maintain data quality, metadata, and lineage.
- **Solution**:
    - Implement data catalogs, lineage tracking, and automated data quality checks.
    - Adopt master data management (MDM) practices for consistent reference data across departments.

12.5.2 Model Proliferation

- **Issue**: Multiple teams might train countless models that overlap in function or degrade without maintenance.
- **Solution**:
    - Maintain a **model registry** to track versioning, usage, and ownership.
    - Periodically prune, retire, or consolidate models that no longer provide value.

12.5.3 Cultural Resistance at Scale

- **Issue**: Early AI adopters may embrace experimentation, but scaling can face skepticism from departments new to AI.
- **Solution**:
    - Conduct workshops, share success stories, and create incentive structures that reward data-driven innovation.
    - Encourage a "fail fast, learn faster" mindset, ensuring mistakes are seen as learning opportunities.

12.5.4 Regulatory Complexity

- **Issue**: Operating in multiple countries or industries (finance, healthcare, etc.) introduces varied rules on data handling and AI usage.
- **Solution**:
    - Establish a **compliance team** to keep pace with evolving legislation and adapt AI systems accordingly.
    - Use built-in compliance features from major cloud providers where appropriate.

12.6Future-Proofing Your AI Strategy

- **Monitor Emerging Tech:** Stay current with breakthroughs in **generative AI**, **reinforcement learning**, **quantum computing**, and more, assessing if they can offer a competitive edge.
- **R&D Investments:** Allocating a portion of budget to research encourages ongoing experimentation, prototyping, and early adoption of novel techniques.
- **Ecosystem Partnerships:** Partner with startups, universities, and industry consortia to co-develop solutions or tap into specialized talent.
- **Focus on Human Skills:**As automation handles repetitive tasks, cultivate creativity, empathy, and leadership capabilities within your workforce.
- **Renew Ethical Commitments:** Larger scale = greater social impact. Regularly review **bias detection, transparency** measures, and **accountability** protocols to maintain trust.

12.7 Looking Ahead

Scaling AI is a marathon, not a sprint. By harmonizing **infrastructure**, **teams**, **processes**, and **governance**, organizations can evolve from isolated pilots to a **culture where AI consistently drives strategic decisions and innovation**. The final chapter will look at the **future outlook of AI**, synthesizing emerging trends and concluding thoughts on how to remain agile, ethical, and competitive in a rapidly changing landscape.

Key Takeaways

- **Scaling AI Extends Impact**: Moving beyond departmental pilots multiplies AI's value, transforming entire business models and operational flows.
- **Foundational Elements**: Well-structured data platforms, robust MLOps, and standardized governance are must-haves for stable, scalable AI.
- **Organizational Models**: Center of Excellence, hub-and-spoke, or fully distributed teams - choose the structure that best fits your size, culture, and regulatory environment.
- **Avoiding Growing Pains**: Plan for data overload, model proliferation, cultural resistance, and regulatory hurdles as your AI footprint expands.
- **Future-Proofing**: Continuous learning, investment in emerging tech, strong ethics, and a focus on human skills keep organizations ahead of the curve.

When *AI maturity* grows beyond localized experiments, it becomes a dynamic, evolving capability that reshapes how an organization competes, innovates, and serves its stakeholders - now and for years to come.

CHAPTER 13

The Road to Advanced AI

"AI's evolution has only just begun. Today's breakthroughs in machine learning, deep learning, and LLMs will seem rudimentary tomorrow as we push toward more adaptive, interactive, and human-centric systems."

From the early days of symbolic AI to the sophisticated deep learning applications transforming businesses, AI's journey has been marked by **rapid innovation** and **expanding horizons**. Yet the current wave of AI solutions - while impressive - only scratches the surface of what's possible. In this penultimate chapter, we'll explore emerging trends and advanced techniques that could reshape industries once again, discuss the skills needed to adapt, and ponder how to **stay on the cutting edge**.

13.1 Emerging Trends in AI

13.1.1 Reinforcement Learning in Real-World Applications

- **What It Is**: Algorithms that learn optimal behaviors through **trial and error**, receiving rewards for positive outcomes and penalties for negative ones.
- **Potential**: Beyond game-playing (Go, StarCraft), RL can optimize logistics routes, robotic control systems, and dynamic pricing strategies.
- **Challenge**: Requires carefully designed reward functions and can be data-hungry. Real-world environments often present high complexity and risk (e.g., self-driving cars in city traffic).

13.1.2 Foundation and Large Language Models (LLMs)

- **What They Are**: Enormous neural networks (e.g., GPT-series models) pre-trained on vast text corpora, then fine-tuned for specific tasks.
- **Potential**:
    - Automating content generation, summarizing complex legal or medical documents.
    - Acting as conversational agents in customer service or as brainstorming partners in creative industries.
- **Challenge**:
    - Managing **hallucinations** (LLMs confidently provide incorrect information).
    - Ensuring **factuality**, **security**, and **compliance** when these models handle sensitive data.

13.1.3 Multimodal AI

- **What It Is**: Models that simultaneously process **text, images, audio,** and possibly other data (e.g., sensors, video) to form holistic insights.
- **Potential**:
    - A single AI system that can understand a document, interpret images, and process spoken language, improving accuracy and user experience.
- **Challenge**: Requires even **larger datasets** and **robust architectures** to handle heterogeneous inputs.

13.1.4 Neuro-Symbolic AI

- **What It Is**: Approaches combining **symbolic reasoning** (logic-based, interpretable) with **neural networks** (pattern recognition).
- **Potential**:
    - Achieve both **high accuracy** and **explainability** - a "best-of-both-worlds" scenario.
    - Useful in domains needing rigorous logic alongside complex data patterns (e.g., legal reasoning, engineering design).

- **Challenge**: Creating effective integrations that don't revert to brittle, rule-based systems while still gaining the interpretability benefits.

13.1.5 Quantum Machine Learning

- **What It Is**: Leveraging **quantum computing** principles to solve certain ML problems faster than classical computers (in theory).
- **Potential**:
    - Accelerate combinatorial optimization, cryptography, and large-scale data analysis.
- **Challenge**: **Practical quantum computers** with enough qubits and low error rates are still in development. Widespread applications remain mostly **research-focused** for now.

13.2 The Evolving Skill Set

13.2.1 Deep Technical Expertise

- **Ongoing Education:**
    - Data scientists and ML engineers must keep up with new frameworks (PyTorch, JAX, etc.) and advanced architectures (transformers, graph neural networks).
- **Mathematics & Theoretical Foundations**:
    - As models become more complex, a solid understanding of linear algebra, probability, and optimization remains crucial.

13.2.2 Domain-Specific Knowledge

- Vertical Specialization:
    - AI in healthcare requires medical domain expertise; AI in finance demands familiarity with trading, risk management, compliance, etc.
- Hybrid Roles:
    - "Analytics Translators" or "Machine Learning Product Managers" bridge the gap between cutting-edge models and the specific needs of their industries.

13.2.3 Ethical and Regulatory Acumen

- Navigating New Rules:
    - Proposed regulations like the EU AI Act or updates to existing laws (GDPR expansions) require legal-technical interplay.
- Responsible Deployment:
    - Skills in model explainability, fairness auditing, bias mitigation, and user consent design will be in high demand.

13.2.4 Soft Skills and Creativity

- Human-Machine Collaboration:
    - AI can automate routine tasks, freeing professionals to focus on creative strategy, empathy-driven services, and complex decision-making.
- Communication & Storytelling:
    - Translating advanced AI insights into business-ready narratives will remain a differentiator for AI-savvy professionals and leaders.

13.3 Strategies to Stay on the Cutting Edge

Continuous Learning Culture

- Encourage team members to pursue online courses, attend conferences, and participate in hackathons.
- Allocate **innovation time** - like Google's "20% time" - for employees to explore novel AI ideas.

Active Participation in Open Source and Research Communities

- Contribute to projects on GitHub, engage with Kaggle competitions, or publish findings in peer-reviewed journals.
- This not only hones skills but also fosters a reputation as a forward-thinking organization.

Collaborative Partnerships

- **Academia**: Sponsor university research projects or offer internships to students working on frontier AI problems.
- **Startups**: Invest in or incubate early-stage AI ventures, tapping into disruptive innovations.

Pilot Advanced Technologies

- Evaluate the feasibility of new techniques - like reinforcement learning or neuro-symbolic AI - through **controlled experiments**.
- Scale up successful pilots to production, maintaining a feedback loop to refine approaches.

Global Perspective

- AI breakthroughs occur worldwide - keep an eye on innovations from China, the EU, India, and emerging tech hubs in Africa or South America.
- Embrace **cultural and linguistic diversity** in data and design to create truly global AI solutions.

13.4 Balancing Innovation with Responsibility

13.4.1 Ethical AI as a Continuous Commitment

- **Ongoing Audits**: As models evolve or new data streams come online, keep re-checking bias, privacy compliance, and accountability frameworks.
- **User Trust**: Innovative AI that drastically impacts user experiences - like always-on personal assistants - demands **transparent** user policies and robust security.

13.4.2 Regulatory and Societal Shifts

- **Flexible Architecture**: Design AI systems to adapt quickly to new or updated regulations.

- **Public Engagement**: Foster open dialogue with stakeholders and user communities, pre-empting concerns around privacy, job displacement, or algorithmic bias.

13.5 Toward More Human-Centric AI

While future AI might become more autonomous - capable of reasoning or creativity beyond what we envision today - it's equally clear that **humanity's moral and emotional compass** must remain central. The next generation of AI solutions will likely focus on:

- **Assistive Intelligence**: Tools that augment human capability without displacing the empathy and nuanced judgment only people can provide.
- **Collaborative Robots (Cobots)**: Machines that safely share workspaces with humans, adjusting actions based on real-time feedback and context.
- **Inclusive Design**: Interfaces and functionalities mindful of diverse user needs - accessibility, multilingual support, and cultural sensitivity.

13.6 Looking Ahead to the Final Chapter

In the final chapter, we'll **summarize the key insights** from this book, reiterating the themes of **responsible AI adoption, organizational alignment, and continuous innovation**. We'll also provide a **call to action** for business leaders, technologists, and policy-makers, urging them to seize AI's potential for positive global impact while guarding against its risks.

Key Takeaways

- **AI Is Rapidly Evolving**: Breakthroughs in reinforcement learning, LLMs, multimodal models, neuro-symbolic AI, and quantum computing promise to redefine the field.
- **Skill Sets Must Expand**: Beyond technical prowess, practitioners need domain expertise, ethical insight, and soft skills to thrive in next-gen AI roles.

- **Continuous Innovation**: Organizations that foster a culture of learning, research, and experimentation will remain competitive amidst technological shifts.
- **Responsible Deployment**: Advanced AI can amplify benefits but also magnify risks. Ongoing ethical audits, stakeholder engagement, and compliance structures are crucial.
- **Human-Centric Future**: The ultimate goal is AI that **enhances** human abilities - collaborating with us instead of replacing our core strengths in empathy, creativity, and ethical judgment.

The road to **Advanced AI** is as much about anticipating future challenges as it is about seizing new opportunities. By staying curious, investing in robust governance, and nurturing interdisciplinary talent, you can ensure that your AI journey remains both **cutting-edge** and **human-focused**.

CONCLUSION

Embracing AI for Sustainable Success

"AI's greatest promise lies in its ability to extend human potential - enabling us to solve complex problems, unlock innovation, and shape a future that balances profit, ethics, and societal good."

Over the course of this book, we've journeyed through the evolution of Artificial Intelligence - from foundational concepts and team structures to real-world applications and the ethical frameworks needed to ensure responsible deployment. We've also explored how organizations progress in their **AI maturity**, how data science lifecycles drive continual improvement, and the crucial interplay between **business strategy, math, data,** and **technology**. Finally, we looked at what lies on the horizon for **advanced AI** - from reinforcement learning to quantum computing - and how to adapt to these fast-moving frontiers responsibly.

14.1 Recap of Key Insights

AI Is a Strategic Asset: No longer a "nice-to-have," AI has become essential for businesses aiming to stay competitive. It provides data-driven insights, automates routine tasks, and expands the possibilities for product and service innovation.

Human Intelligence Remains Irreplaceable: Despite AI's capabilities, human empathy, creativity, and ethical judgment remain crucial. True success emerges from **human + AI** collaborations, where each complements the other's strengths.

Ethical AI Is Non-Negotiable: Bias, privacy, transparency, and accountability are not theoretical concerns; they are practical imperatives. A culture of responsible AI ensures that technology benefits *all stakeholders*, not just a privileged few.

Scaling AI Requires Robust Infrastructure and Governance: Moving beyond pilot projects demands reliable data pipelines, MLOps, and clear organizational structures (CoE, hub-and-spoke, etc.). Frequent model retraining and monitoring maintain relevance in changing environments.

Continuous Learning and Adaptability: The pace of AI innovation is relentless. Both individuals and organizations must embrace ongoing education, open dialogue, and flexible strategies to leverage the latest breakthroughs effectively.

Collaboration Is the Core: Cross-functional teams - spanning business strategy, data engineering, data science, and technical operations - drive AI projects to meaningful, value-generating outcomes.

14.2 A Call to Action: Building Sustainable AI Competencies

14.2.1 For Business Leaders

Align AI with Vision: Define how AI supports your broader strategic goals - whether increasing revenue, enhancing customer experiences, or improving operational efficiency. Make sure each AI initiative has clear ROI metrics, executive sponsorship, and a roadmap for adoption.

Invest in People: Develop internal talent through training, mentorship, and rotating team members into AI projects. Recruit diverse voices - both technologists and domain experts - who can guide ethical and impactful solutions.

Champion an Ethical Culture: Set up governance committees or designate responsible AI leads. Encourage open discussions about data, privacy, fairness, and the societal impact of AI deployments.

14.2.2 For Technologists and Data Scientists

Stay Curious and Current: AI tools and frameworks evolve constantly. Pursue continuous learning through courses, research papers, coding challenges, and community forums. Experiment with emerging techniques (reinforcement learning, large language models, neuro-symbolic AI) to keep skills sharp.

Master the Full Lifecycle: Understand data collection, cleaning, feature engineering, modeling, and deployment. Communicate insights clearly to stakeholders, bridging the gap between complex algorithms and real business needs.

Build with Responsibility: Proactively test for bias, ensure data is handled ethically, and document the assumptions and limitations of each model. Collaborate with business owners and subject matter experts to ensure your solutions align with practical, user-centric outcomes.

14.2.3 For Policy Makers and Regulators

Balance Innovation and Oversight: Craft regulations that protect citizens from unethical or harmful AI practices without stifling beneficial innovation. Engage with industry stakeholders, researchers, and civil society to form nuanced policies.

Promote Accessibility and Fairness: Support open data initiatives, fund public AI research, and encourage AI education across socioeconomic backgrounds. Seek global cooperation to harmonize AI standards and address cross-border challenges like data sharing and digital rights.

Continuously Adapt: Remain agile as AI technology matures. Regularly update legislation and guidelines to reflect new capabilities and threats (deepfakes, advanced surveillance, etc.).

14.3 Sustaining Momentum and Looking Ahead

The journey doesn't end once you've deployed a few AI projects or reached a certain maturity level. Technology evolves, business landscapes shift, and new ethical questions surface as AI becomes increasingly integrated into society. Staying at the forefront of responsible AI demands:

Ongoing Innovation: Encourage R&D and experimental "moonshot" projects that might unlock breakthrough products or processes. Partner with academic institutions, open-source communities, and industry consortia for fresh ideas.

Feedback Loops and Measurement: Continuously gather insights from end-users and cross-functional teams. Refine your AI systems, retrain models, and pivot strategies when results deviate from expectations or user needs evolve.

Future-Proofing Skills and Ethics: As automation and AI reshape job roles, invest in workforce development: upskill, reskill, and cultivate human-centric skills like empathy, ethics, and creative problem-solving.

Global Perspective: AI is borderless; adopt a global mindset by learning from technological advances and policy trends around the world. Explore emerging markets, adapt to diverse cultural contexts, and shape AI solutions that respect different local norms and regulations.

14.4 Final Thoughts

AI stands at the intersection of technology, society, and humanity. While its possibilities are vast - driving unprecedented efficiency, personalization, and problem-solving - its challenges are equally formidable. Ensuring **AI remains a force for good** requires collective effort: visionary leadership, responsible governance, technical excellence, and ethical vigilance.

By combining **data-driven innovation** with **compassion, creativity, and accountability**, you can harness AI's transformative power without losing sight of the very people it intends to serve. Let this book be your guide - a roadmap that shows not just *what AI is* and *how it works*, but also *why it matters* and *where it's going*. The next chapter of AI's story will be written by those who take these insights, build upon them, and forge new paths toward a future that's both advanced and profoundly human.

You hold the pen. Write boldly, responsibly, and with a vision that extends beyond mere efficiency to truly sustainable, equitable success.

Key Takeaways

- **AI Is Both Tool and Vision**: It's not merely a technical project, but an organizational and societal endeavor requiring strategic thinking and a clear moral compass.

- **Sustainability Over Hype**: True success emerges when AI projects are ethically grounded, thoroughly integrated, and continuously improved - beyond initial proofs of concept.
- **Cross-Disciplinary Collaboration**: Effective AI adoption is a team sport that unites business leaders, data scientists, engineers, ethicists, and regulators.
- **Perpetual Evolution**: AI technology, best practices, and regulations shift rapidly. Maintain agility, keep learning, and remain open to transformative ideas.
- **Human-Centric Future**: The ultimate measure of AI's value is its **positive impact on people** - enhancing creativity, well-being, and global prosperity.

ABOUT THE AUTHOR

Mohamed Fawzi Elgendi

I, Mohamed Fawzi Elgendi, have dedicated over 15 years to the dynamic fields of information security, digital innovation, and artificial intelligence. Serving as both a Chief Digital and AI Officer and a Chief Information Security Officer (CISO), I've been fortunate to spearhead significant technological advancements. My academic foundation is built upon a bachelor's degree in computer and systems engineering, complemented by a postgraduate program in Artificial Intelligence for Leaders.

My professional capabilities are broad, encompassing software development, IT operations, and the latest AI technologies. This extensive experience has allowed me to effectively navigate today's complex digital environments. In my roles, I emphasize the critical integration of strong security measures into digital transformation strategies, viewing security as essential for fostering innovation. I have successfully created and put into action comprehensive security frameworks that protect organizations from the constantly changing landscape of cyber threats, while also promoting a culture of ongoing improvement and flexibility.

My commitment extends beyond my professional duties to include a deep passion for youth empowerment. This passion led to the establishment of the Fawzooz Initiative, which aims to provide cultural and educational resources to young people, preparing them for success in our increasingly digital world.

As a thought leader, I am proactive in sharing my perspectives on the intersection of technology, AI, and security. I engage in speaking engagements, contribute to various publications, and maintain an active presence on my website, www.fawzooz.ai. My professional philosophy is centered on the belief that effective digital leadership, combined with stringent security practices, is crucial for organizational success in today's fast-paced technological era. Whether driving digital innovation or advocating for robust security strategies, I am dedicated to influencing the trajectory of technology and cybersecurity.

www.ingramcontent.com/pod-product-compliance
Lightning Source LLC
LaVergne TN
LVHW090416210926
848480LV00002B/589